LINCOLN CHRISTIAN

W9-BRR-052

# Teaching Students To Teach Themselves

Crawford W. Lindsey, Jr.

NP

Nichols Publishing/New York
Kogan Page/London

First published in 1988 by Nichols Publishing,
P.O. Box 96, New York, NY 10024

© 1988 by GP Publishing, Inc.
  All rights reserved

Books bearing the Nichols Publishing imprint are published by GP Publishing,
Inc.

**Library of Congress Cataloging-in-Publication Data**

Lindsey, Crawford
    Teaching students to teach themselves / by Crawford W. Linsey, Jr.
    p. cm.
    Bibliography: p.
    1. Teaching. 2. Education—United States—Experimental methods.
3. Group work in education. 4. Critical thinking—Study and
teaching—United States. I. Title.
    LB1027.3.L56 1988                                      88-11026
    371.1'02—dc19                                          CIP

Published in the United Kingdom by Kogan Page, Ltd, 120 Pentonville Road,
London N1 9JN

**British Library Cataloguing in Publication Data**
Lindsey, Jr., Crawford W.
    Teaching students to teach themselves.
    1. Teaching methods—Manuals
    I. Title
    371.3

    ISBN 1-85091-662-4

Printed and bound in the United States of America
94 93 92 91 90 89 88        5 4 3 2 1

# Contents

# Introduction

This book was borne out of a feeling of complete isolation. Even though thirty people were sitting in front of me, I felt utterly alone. These thirty would leave, and thirty more would come in. It did not make much difference who they were—I would perform the same rituals with the same results. I began to feel trapped inside myself, as if I were talking but no one could hear me. I felt simultaneously as if I were invisible and as if I were performing without an audience. I heard the same words, ideas, interpretations, and conclusions over and over, class after class. They were always the same. Nothing evolved.

I wanted to scream, jump up and down, wave hysterically—"Is anybody out there? Please answer. Confirm my existence. Confirm yours." A heavy, seemingly impenetrable wall of silence stood between myself and them, and I feared that my nightmarish reality was a solipsistic creation in which I was an eternal prisoner.

Many teachers have experienced this feeling. But what can we do about it? How can we transform the performing stage of the classroom into an arena where there is no, or at least much less, distinction between the audience and the action? This book is an answer to that question.

One frustration with relying on the predominating lecture-authoritarian-noninteractive teaching methods is that teachers seldom see any proof of individuals evolving. Students are always just sitting there. Multidimensional evidence that a vital idea world exists within their heads is rare, and we do not have the time or the resources to witness one if it does occur. Sometimes, in an attempt to correct this situation, we try to have a class discussion—a meeting and opening of minds, so to speak. On my first attempt at this, I was appalled: the students demonstrated an almost total inability to speak and think in such a setting. I was shocked to think that *these* performances, not grades on a fill-in-the-blank test, were the true reflections of students' thinking processes.

If my perception is correct, a completely new emphasis is needed. Each of the many thinking skills uses the brain differently but always in an interactive, complementary, and reinforcing way. There has to be a teaching method to get all these skills working, practicing, performing, and growing. There has to be a method that creates a situation in which every person is continually thinking and working in a socially interactive setting. Such a method requires multidimensional planning, multidimensional learning, and multidimensional performance. This book offers a method that is a first step in this direction—teaching students to teach themselves.

What does this method involve? Quite simply, it is a classroom technique in which students do all the researching, organizing, teaching, and grading, as well as attend to their usual student responsibilities. This approach is accomplished by dividing the class into groups of approximately six persons and redistributing the teacher's roles and duties among the students of each group. Each group becomes a miniclass, each simultaneously in session along with the others, and each with its own teacher or teachers. This format is organized by activities that dictate what will be studied, who will be responsible for what and when, what the speaking, writing, organizing, and evaluating duties will be, and what kind of skills, apart from the content, will be emphasized.

This method is outlined in the following pages, as are guidelines for implementation in any classroom, subject, or grade, with one qualification: the principles, structure, and organization of each exercise are applicable to any classroom, subject, or grade, although the particular exercise itself may not be. The cases presented here are oriented toward high school social studies classes. The basic principles are the same in every case, however; only the content must be changed.

This book is divided into two parts. The first is a philosophical rationale for the detailed activities of the second. It begins with a somewhat lighthearted fictitious account of my observations of the proceedings in a stereotypical class. Using this experience as a starting point, it proceeds to analyze the shortcomings of traditional classroom teaching methods and builds a case for an alternative—teaching students to teach themselves.

The second part presents six activities that can be used as the foundation for such a teaching method. These activities, including their elements, methods, organizations, results, and ramifications, are discussed in detail. The second part is the practical result of the thinking in the first part. It grounds the first part in reality and addresses the problems brought to light there. Together, these parts present a comprehensive introduction to an exciting, new teaching method that will free students and teachers alike from the confining roles that impede true multidimensional learning.

**Part 1
Why?**

# 1

## Points
## of Departure

How are unbounded excitement about ideas and unquench-able desire for knowledge expressed? Are they visible on the faces of these students as they stare back at me? Are they to be seen in the wrinkling of the brow, squinting of the eyes, tightly pursed lips, and erect posture? Or should I be looking for a certain sparkle in the eye and a mouth half smiling, half agape, revealing both joy and wonder? Or perhaps they are to be found in slumped, lifeless bodies crowned with expression-less faces. Somewhere behind each of those faces lies the mean-ing of education.

These were my initial, fleeting impressions on first stand-ing behind the lectern in a high school social science class. Soon the business at hand erased those faces from my mind, and I was just talking. The faces merged into one—the "class"—and all learning was depersonalized after that point.

Depersonalization is not one of the ultimate objectives of the public school system. Instead, the acclaimed objectives are those that will produce self-actualized, caring, creative, imagi-native, motivated, curious, adventurous, sharing, communi-cating, socially responsible, globally aware, and intelligent human beings. Is this transformation occurring anywhere in our educational system? Is the system set up to accomplish these goals? Are American theories of teaching and learning adequate to the task? Are teachers' techniques appropriate for eliciting the sought-after behaviors? Is there a better way? Let's sit in on a class to see.

# A Visit to the Classroom

Sitting in the back of the classroom, trying to look inconspicuous, I wait for the class to be called to order. As I look around, I wonder whether such a thing can be done. Youth in its most effervescent stage is bubbling before me. Everyone knows everyone else, and it seems that each person is trying to talk to everyone else at once. Quieting this group would be like trying to stop water from boiling without taking it from the heat. In the students' case the heat is generated from within and there is no knob to turn it off. To my surprise the class is called to order, and the lesson begins.

After a few preliminaries—instructions and passing in of homework—the class moves into its habitual pattern. The teacher is lecturing. Some students are taking notes; others are passing notes. Some are listening; others are daydreaming. I cannot help launching into a daydream of my own.

I rocket through memory space until I arrive back in first grade. It is my birthday, and I have a new watch—my first one. I am watching the second hand mark out the time, and I fondle and smell the leather wristband. Am I pondering the significance of birthdays and their connection to time? Probably not. Mrs. Benson, the teacher, classifies my behavior as "inattentive" and sends me to the corner. Ironically, this pronouncement releases me from the structure that defines the pursuit of my curiosities as "nonpursuit." I am happy to be in the corner, for now I can pay undivided attention to my new watch. I am thinking, What does "inattentive" mean, anyway? What is wrong with Mrs. Benson?

With this question, the "inattentive" one vanished back into the darkness of memory, and I returned to the present, with a new perspective on the confrontational relationship between teaching and learning that is implicitly built into the educational system. One of the main rationalizations accepted in education is that students do not learn because they are unruly, inattentive, and unmotivated. But this diagnosis seems to be misdirected. Looking at the class before me—of youth growing into its form, realizing its potential, becoming—I realize that most of the difficulties students have with learning do not result from their own problems or characteristics but from problems the system has laid on them. Could it be that we unknowingly project the faults of our teaching system on the students and then consider this projection a true indication of what students are like.

A good analogy of our attributing "problems" to students is the maze-running laboratory rat. Our treatment of children is similar to putting a rat in a maze for the first time and then proclaiming it either a "good" or "bad" maze runner. If it is a bad maze runner, there is nothing the matter with it, for the maze and its attendant "cultural determinants" certainly are not the rat's natural habitat or the one most suited to demonstrate its real abilities. We do not have to look for the causes of this "inability" in some physiological or psychological shortcoming, injury, or lack. Certainly the rat is not unmotivated, inattentive, or undisciplined. Nor do we have to make up a category of identification such as "maze-a-pepsia" in order to treat the "disorder." The problem comes from us; we project it onto the rat. Certainly there is no reason why the rat would get overly excited about running the maze for its own sake.

But for our purposes—the experimenter's purpose—the rat must run, and in order to ensure that it does, we place a tasty tidbit of cheese at the other end of the maze—a reward for doing what it certainly would not have done otherwise. We arrange our conceptualizations in such a manner that soon, to us, a rat exists simply to run the maze and has maze-running ability built into it. If it does not demonstrate this ability, something is wrong with it, so we send the rat to the corner.

Most of we teachers behaved the same way in high school—we were somewhat inattentive, uninterested, or unmotivated—but after a few years of college or graduate work, we forgot that earlier behavior. We became part and parcel of the system and now lament the fact that high school students are not. What we see happening to the students today has already happened to us. They are our selves of the past; we are our children of the future. Does this bode well for the future or speak ill of the present? Should we continue to measure people in terms of the needs of the system, or should we measure the system in terms of the needs of the people?

It is getting on toward the middle of the period now, and the class is becoming more restless. There is a constant rustling sound, like the wind blowing through the leaves. At this point I wonder what information is actually being assimilated by the students and what intellectual processes they are using to integrate that information. Is this lecture effectively communicating to the class? Is it helping achieve the ultimate education objectives? Or are the leaves of thought drifting away on restless winds? A powerful urge comes over me to stop the class in its tracks and to ask each student what he or she is thinking at that second. I have a feeling that the teacher has been talking to herself.

Another question I want to ask these students is what they feel are the most important lessons the educational system should be teaching. In fact, I did this once. The students' responses—the meaning of life, peace, happiness, and selfhood—coincided with the teacher's ultimate objectives, but unfortunately the students did not feel that these objectives were taught at all.

What is lacking in our teaching methods and our philosophy of education that such a failure could occur? Our curriculum development assumes that the student will be able to extract these types of lessons by assimilating knowledge of various subjects; after all, these lessons are implicit in the study of such subjects as social studies, literature, and science. The problem is that all the topics listed by the students are holistic concepts requiring a synthesis of the content of all courses as well as self- and social development, whereas teachers often present subjects in a fragmented and independent manner to quiet students isolated in their seating chart locations. Education as currently structured is inappropriate for teaching about such issues as life, self, peace, and happiness. In educating ourselves, we have forsaken learning about these things for learning about things of a different, less experiential order. Learning has become separated from experience, structured, and prescribed.

As the rigid education structure continually blocks the pathways of spontaneous and playful inquiry, it simultaneously attempts to divert that energy into taming the student, like the rat, into receiving the "required" information. Most of this energy is devoted to restraint, not to learning. Restraint is used to keep order, but this order masks the reality of what students are actually learning, interested in, and giving attention. To impose order only hides the symptoms of an underlying disease. Worse, the only person from whom they are hidden is the teacher, not the student, who now suffers even more.

As I watch the class slowly show signs of deterioration, I wonder if there is any point in continuing the charade. Not much learning is going on here—certainly not with regard to the ultimate objectives. Even those students who are attentive are so out of fear of punishment or desire for good grades; they are learning by gritting their teeth and biting their tongues. But even as the students retreat into worlds of their own, the teacher continues to strafe the class with rapid fire from her machine-gun-like lecture. Facts are ricocheting all about the room, but the bombardment is largely futile. Occasionally a student makes a note of one of these facts, but a permanent change in behavior is highly improbable.

We teachers maintain this charade by several proven methods:

1. *Dominating conversation.* As long as you are talking, especially if feeding students with "necessary" facts (they'll be on the test!), you will be in control. Not much will go wrong; that is, you will not allow students to behave in the way to which they are naturally inclined in that situation—to ignore

you, to talk to their friends, to leave the room. If you keep talking, the illusion of what you are supposed to be doing—teaching—cannot be destroyed because you do not give the students an opportunity to demonstrate the inadequacy and inappropriateness of your teaching. If you ask them a thought-provoking question but get no response, just keep talking to save yourself embarrassment, discomfort, and tension.

2. *Films and filmstrips.* These are excellent ways to facilitate our jobs by creating the outward appearance of students assimilating knowledge. If we inquire further whether any actual learning is taking place, we are armed with excuses: "What can we do? We give them the material; they just don't do anything with it."

3. *Worksheets.* Again, keep the students busy. The rationale of the worksheet is to solidify memorization of facts read for homework. But since students do not do the homework, then worksheets can be used to say, "See, if you did the reading, this would be easy." The worksheet is supposed to teach them to do the reading. The message: read the boring assignment, and the boring worksheet will be easier. But is the point of reading to be able to do worksheets well and pass tests? If so, no wonder students do not put much effort into either.

Perhaps these activities keep them busy, but the true student in us all rebels at such mindless, work-making activity. Honest teachers know it is mindless, but they are trying to survive the charade that they are imparting valuable knowledge and that the students are actually gobbling it up.

The option that most often raises its head is the traditional lecture-discipline model. At every juncture it presents itself as the only one that will mold children into students. The appearance and the actuality of being a teacher are two completely different things, but teachers are trained and forced into attaining only the appearance. The tragedy is that appearance fools almost everyone because its dominance has blinded us to other ways of thinking.

# Upside-Down Objectives

Again, what is the point of continuing the charade? Although the education objectives always state that the ultimate goal is to teach thinking skills, foster personal growth, and help students form a clear self-concept, these objectives are never actually achieved. The educational system does have multiple objectives, but the ultimate objectives are the least addressed. In fact, the system is organized in such a way as to preclude these goals. At best, they are infrequently and indirectly sneaked into the lessons. If these values are supposed to be taught, why don't we teach them? The entire educational system is upside down. The emphasis must be reversed. At present there is no reason to believe that students will attain any of these so-called objectives except by chance. A student "catches" his or her positive self-concept almost by accident, as if catching cold.

What would happen if we stressed more humane environments, personal growth, social awareness, thinking skills, and experiences—that is, if we strove to achieve our ultimate objectives? If we actually concentrated on those stated goals of personhood, could we produce better-functioning, better-adjusted, more humane, alive, spontaneous, interesting, and motivated individuals who could take more responsibility for their learning and thus learn more, more thoroughly, and more purposefully?

Looking at the class now, as the period draws to a close, I am shocked. Is this the same class I earlier compared to boiling water? The teacher has done the impossible: she has turned these energetic, vigorous, and expressive students into listless, bored, apathetic clock watchers. The energetic and enthusiastic students now sit slumped in their chairs, suffocating in the stale intellectual air. Now the restlessness that earlier had been releases of energy has become dying gasps. Watching this, my own head nodding with weariness, I realize that this energy must somehow be tapped and utilized in the learning process.

The word *learning* evokes several common connotations:

- Learning is forced.
- Learning is passive.
- Learning is no fun.
- Learning is a step to a goal (grades, jobs, or success).
- Learning is required.

These misperceptions become attached to all types of learning thereafter. Is it any wonder that so many people stop actively seeking to learn after it is no longer required?

How has learning come to take on these connotations? It happens as follows. As teachers we examine what happens when children learn, develop concepts about the process, and then turn around and try to *make* the children learn. We try to make them do what they are already doing and teach them by methods they taught us. To try to facilitate the learning process is fine, but the problem is that we have preempted it and have relocated the locus of control. We have taken the natural process from the children, "improved" it, and then tried to force it back down their throats. What would happen if we returned control of the learning to the learners? Given their natural curiosity and motivation and given the raw materials, could they, by themselves, take the information and create entire new universes of knowledge?

At last, the bell. The students slowly rouse themselves, as from a midday nap, and file out of the classroom. Once in the hall, beyond the invisible limits of the teacher's soporific domain, perpetual motion starts anew.

**2**

## Goals

Is there a way to transcend the usual conception of what is involved in teaching and learning—an all-knowing, expert teacher transmitting everything he or she knows to thirty or so students, who then record it verbatim in their memory banks—and to return control of the learning process to the learner? If there is, will it be more effective in achieving our ultimate goals?

The program described in the following chapters presents a system of learning in which all the teacher's roles and duties are redistributed among the students. Each class is divided into groups or miniclasses of about six students, all in independent session at once. The students do all the researching, organizing, explaining, speaking, questioning, testing, grading, writing, and reading. In short, the students perform all the steps involved in thinking and communicating ideas—not just mechanical, nonthinking memorization. All this is done within a structure set up by the teacher that is aimed at having every student participate every day for the entire period. Each student is both a teacher and learner every day, and the amount of meaningful work that is produced dwarfs anything previously thought possible.

The role of the teacher remains extremely important in all these activities. Although the students do the teaching, this activity is not a free ride for the teacher. The teacher's personal knowledge of the students will be much greater than in any other method of classroom organization, and he or she will thus come to know better their abilities, shortcomings, likes, and dislikes. This knowledge comes from carefully observing each student every day in constant classroom *performance,* not from a one-dimensional test paper that periodically floats across the teacher's desk. The teacher can locate students' difficulties every day and design activities to improve those problems. Then, with all this knowledge of the students at hand, the teacher orchestrates student interactions so that the strengths and weaknesses of each student will be matched with those of every other student in ways that will maximize each person's learning and development.

The activities described here and included in later chapters are based on three major assumptions:

1. Teachers must train students in all facets of thinking (in the broadest sense of the word) and do it continuously in an organized and planned program.

2. Teachers must teach social and communication skills and provide opportunities for continual social interaction. That is, the students will be giving to and receiving from many people, not just the teacher, during the entire period.

3. The ultimate aim of all our teaching should be twofold: to develop self-actualized human beings and to work for a better world for everyone.

Notice that *content* is not mentioned here. Content is included, of course, but is only a means to an end, not the end itself. In this case our end—the three assumptions—is to have individuals with fully developed intellectual skills actively participating in a socially interactive community engaged in creating a better world. Such an end includes many more facets of human existence in a mutually reinforcing pattern of interaction: individual, social, and global. In this way, we set up conditions that do not cut off or stifle any part of our being.

## Teaching Thinking Skills

The first assumption mentioned previously is that the design of any course should be that of a thinking skills course. Every activity, therefore, should be aimed at a particular thinking skill. The course content will be the means of getting at the skill, not vice versa, where the skill is assumed to be a preexisting ability that simply needs some practice (i.e., content); for example, when dividing your course into units, do so on two levels—a skill and a content level.

Example:

| *Skill unit* | *Content unit* (European history) |
|---|---|
| Comparing | 1600s |
| Questioning | 1700s |
| Analyzing | 1800s |
| Summarizing | 1900s |
| Hypothesizing | The future |

In the second unit, for example, you will teach how to get at the content by questioning. (See chapter 5.) You will actually spend periods teaching questioning technique, the levels of questioning, and their use, while you simultaneously teach the content of the 1700s—which is what the questions will address.

The idea that students must be taught particular skills is not new, but what, perhaps, is new is the idea that these skills are the real subject of each class and each activity. Most of the time, teachers concentrate on content, believing that thinking skills will result. But if we teach thinking skills, content emerges as a desirable and necessary side effect. The development of these skills allows students to become lifelong, self-motivated learners capable of learning any content in a meaningful way. They learn not because they are "motived"; motivation is an effect, not a cause.

## Teaching Social Skills

Requiring students to sit passively while teachers do all the thinking and speaking has completely cut students off from one another and from their own self-motivation. We try to promote their participation the best we can given the strictures of single-handedly directing thirty students in a fifty-minute period. But when the situation is teacher dominated, participation and teaching are almost mutually exclusive. Any participation is a mere fraction of the students' day-to-day learning, and such a structure (even in the best cases) can only teach passivity, shyness, self-consciousness, inadequacy, and antisocial behavior. These behaviors are characteristic of most students, and we have *taught* them—not consciously but through our hidden curriculum.

What we have actually and inadvertently taught students from kindergarten through twelfth grade is apparent in their first group work interactions designed for self-initiated discovery and exchange of information of a given content. Given this opportunity, most students are totally confused and unable to complete the task. They simply have not been taught the necessary skills. Most teaching methods stress imposing order, not allowing any disruptive behavior, isolating each person into his or her numbered space, imposing absolute silence, disallowing any personal interaction, and requiring competitive behavior between people who do not know or care about one another. Schools send students out into the world with these same feelings—a sense of anonymity, protective of their isolated personality, fearing authority and shying away from other people, unable to communicate or interact with others except with complete superficiality, and with no conception of who they are, except as they have been artificially labled ("best athlete," "best looking," "most likely to succeed," or "biggest nerd.").

The students' journals of the group activities described in the following chapters reinforced this description of socially alienated students. These introspective writings are required by several of the activities in this book in which students must analyze their teaching performances, the group's performance, and the nature of thinking and learning. The excerpts from the first few days of an activity reflect their apprehension: "I can't do this." "I'm too shy." "I'm not good at speaking." "I can't understand this material." "I'm embarrassed." "I'm afraid of what they will think." "I don't know any of these people. Can't we choose our own groups?" In other words, these excerpts demonstrate a lack of self-confidence and a simple fear of talking to one another. These students, 15-18 years old, were afraid to relate to and interact with other people.

As time passed, the journals began indicating revelations: "I can do it." "I can't believe it—they listened to me." "I learned that my ideas are as good as everyone else's." "I learned that other people have good ideas, too." "I really like these people. I didn't think I would because we are all so different."

What is so shocking is that these ideas really were revelations. Imagine finding out at sixteen years of age that your ideas will not be laughed at and that other people have ideas also. Imagine students discovering for the first time that they can talk to one another.

Without continual practice, these revelations will soon be forgotten. They certainly will not become an unquestioned part of the student's self-concept. But most people never get the opportunity to experience these revelations in the first place. Instead, they remain quietly in their assigned seat for the rest of their lives.

## Teaching for a Better World

Our teaching should be based on a vision of a better world. To this end, we should alter our thinking as teachers: we should not be thinking that we are filling individual heads with knowledge but instead that we are building a social information community. This concept means that we should be enabling people to become communication channels, not simply communication terminals. This need is especially strong in the social studies, in which we are supposed to be helping develop world cooperation and community. We cannot do this by imposing a system of individual isolation with an emphasis on competing with other isolated individuals. When we do not keep this larger purpose of education constantly in mind, our teaching suffers from the loss of ultimate meaning.

A more appropriate education is necessary if students are going to relate in a humane, meaningful, and purposeful way to themselves, other people, and the finite world. It can be argued that at present the world situation is such that many of these relationships are anonymous, self-centered, unecological, and globally destructive. And although we have learned our lessons in school concerning this state of affairs, this "learning" does not stop us from making the same mistakes about which we have read. Why?

Consider this: students do not have much difficulty understanding such concepts as overpopulation, famine and hunger, unemployment, death, nuclear war, and destruction of the biosphere, but they understand them only as concepts. Most students have a great deal of trouble understanding them as actual experiences. They know the definitions of *empathy, compassion, love, help, caring,* and *community,* but there is only one problem—they have not had much opportunity to experience the meaning behind these concepts. The staggering numbers of people starving or the potential deaths locked up within a nuclear warhead evoke exaggerated responses, to be sure, but these are always superficial responses: "Wow! Millions of people live near starvation. That is amazing! I can't even imagine that many people." "If you lined up all the people of China and walked them off a cliff into a bottomless ravine, the line would still get longer because of the high birth rates. Wow! What an incredible concept!"

These are not the reactions of whole human beings because they make no mention of people. These are just mind games, a reaction of only a small part of our being, and they do not get translated into effective action.

The same reaction also occurs on a more personal level. How else can we explain why people stand by and watch muggings or refuse to get involved in "other people's" problems? Why else do we have such difficulty offering and receiving help? Why else do we feel embarrassed when dealing with foreigners and strangers or when confronted with any situation that requires a personal relation that is more profound than superficial niceties such as "Nice day, isn't it?" or"May I help you find something, sir?" The answer is, we don't know how we should behave. We have not had any practice in proper behavior. And those necessary parts of our beings that would enable us to become truly social beings remain locked away somewhere inside ourselves.

Although this goal of education for a world community is the goal of many teachers, the method by which we aim to accomplish it precludes the possibility of our success. Our goals and our methods are mutually contradictory. As a result, we lose sight of our goal, for it seems so far off, and we concentrate on the more immediate goal of information acquisition. This is the most easily measurable sign of "learning" and also the most immediate way for teachers to alleviate their frustration and get some evidence that they are doing something Without measurable proof, we all seem to lose our commitment and identity. We come to feel inadequate, unfulfilled, or insecure in our jobs.

Perhaps this idea of teaching students to teach themselves rests on an act of faith—that students are capable of such a thing—but we must risk this faith if we wish to move toward a more globally humane existence.

**3**

# Rationale

Teachers have been taught how to prepare, organize, and transmit material so that students will understand it. Teachers present the information prepackaged and prewrapped. Students rarely learn how to anayze and synthesize material for themselves because they are always dealing with the end product. Fully developed thinking is not essential—the teacher has done all of that—because to be given information with meaning does not develop the skills to make information meaningful. Instead, students should be taught to do every function that teachers now provide for them. Learning to be a teacher is learning how to learn.

## Learning to Teach is Learning to Learn

To implement this program, the "hidden resources"—the students—must be used to best advantage. Students, not teachers, are the most abundant resource available for implementing the learning process. Even the terms *teacher* and *student* are misleading, implying a counterproductive division of labor. Each person is a "teacher-student." Teachers cannot realize the potential of their accumulated experience for the class unless they use the students as helpers; otherwise they get bogged down in work that students could be gaining from if they were doing it, too. For this reason, this method recommends dividing the class into groups of 2-6 persons, with a different student in each group acting as "teacher" each day, according to the directions of the particular activity (explained in detail in chapters 5-10).

One initial problem is that students are not used to this kind of learning. It is different from their experience in other classes, and they are not likely to see the benefit. At first, they will see it only as upsetting the applecart of everyday habit and expectations. They will not be able to connect it to their usual reward system, which is located outside themselves and defined in such measurements as grades. Success is measured in terms of this external system of rewards, not some less visible, internal, or less measurable system of skills. Students take a course only to fulfill a required credit, and they do not want to have to think in a new way in order to get that credit. They have figured out the system, and they do not want any curves thrown their way that might jolt them out of their safe and familiar sameness.

Obviously, more balance is needed in the education structure. The program presented here is not meant to be a cure-all but to provide more balance. The method will probaby be more amenable to certain disciplines (although it can be used in all). Thus, to provide a balance in thinking skills, these more amenable courses might include many more of these techniques— perhaps to the exclusion of others. The goal is balance across the entire curriculum to which a student is exposed over the years—not just in a particular course.

# Participation

The following activities complement one another. Each builds and expands on the skills acquired through the others, but each approaches them from different directions. The common characteristic of the activities is the students' participation in their own learning. These activities allow students to be who they are while they learn, instead of playing roles that stifle personality (and with it, learning).

The danger in most sorts of activities is that they structure students' behavior and thinking every moment. This program's activities allow attention to wander momentarily and then return, resulting in longevity of attention. Fading in and out allows a student—and the entire group—more freedom to learn. Spontaneous and unpunished "off-task" activity is a necessary respite so that students can concentrate and learn more when they are on task. Laughter is a part of learning. So is dancing around the topic—in and out of the task, back and forth. In this way, students have some self-initiated fun in spite of the material, and they learn the material as a result.

Once they get comfortable and gain control in these ways, then the conditions are set for peer individualization and self-paced learning. The environment also encourages the students to ask questions and even, given an unintimidating opportunity, to show off what they know. A large class is too impersonal and threatening to allow all this to happen. Small groups, on the other hand, relieve tension and vary the stimulus (the "teacher"), which in a class dominated by a single teacher can become soporific.

The contribution of personalities goes even further. In the discussions, students get to know one another as people, not just as other students. The new bonds and friendships inject an extra enthusiasm, a higher energy level, into the discussions. This personal interrelating represents a much deeper level of connectedness than purely intellectual bonds or robotlike, grade-inspired performance.

The small groups magnify a person's individual role in every situation and reveal his or her contribution in unexpected ways. Interaction in a small group is just that—inter*action*. All five people are present to the other five; they contribute by mere presence. In small groups, smiles, posture, statements, eye contact, just sitting—everything—are interaction, because everyone reacts to everything (consciously or unconsciously). Each person cannot help but affect these groups with his or her behavior; thus, the experience becomes personal even if that person does not try to make it so.

To get the most participation possible out of these activities, the students must make a semester-long commitment to group learning. Most people must have a continual opportunity over an extended period of time to accomplish the goals of these activities. Having just a few opportunities a semester is not enough for most people to find themselves, break their inertia of self-consciousness, build confidence, feel comfortable, become a true member, and break the shell of apathy. In fact, the difficulties that usually ensue from infrequent sojourns into group learning are often pointed to as reason enough for not pursuing them. But the truth is, students' lack of understanding is not so obvious when they are silently struggling by themselves, lost in the anonymity of a large, teacher-dominated class, but it is nonetheless real.

The difficulty can itself be seen as a rationale: for the very reason that this type of learning is difficult or seemingly impossible at first, we must pursue more opportunities to develop the skills to make such learning possible.

Infrequent and totally inadequate presentations are a more accurate reflection of students' thinking processes than their performance on a paper or a test. Often they cannot extract the whole picture or the theme from the material they are presenting. They have difficulty interpreting and approaching the material in ways that make it interesting or understandable. They also have difficulty generalizing, analyzing, and applying the material. Most students have difficulty escaping from the bonds of the written word to examine the information from many perspectives besides the imediate one of a mechanical repetition of word sequences. Having completed this performance, they have trouble stepping back from the material in order to summarize what they have just said.

Teachers must help develop the ability to step into higher dimensions of thought so that students can see the entire panorama before them. If we continually lecture them, we could present the main theme and summarize the important points, but being told these themes will never help them find themes on their own. Coupled with the exercises, the presentations serve this purpose: by teaching the material to others, students become much more aware of their own reading, writing, speaking, and thinking. To explain a concept to someone involves examining one's own thinking processes for clues about how to organize and reorganize information.

## Individualization and Maximization

Constant interaction with other people reveals a great deal about their abilities, potentials, and personalities. Thus, it provides an opportunity to develop diagnostic, prescriptive, and challenging lessons and activities for the students. With this method you see each student in constant interaction and performance, not just a few assigned or coerced performances in a teacher-dominated setting.

In any class, students have varying levels of ability. When a teacher deals with a class as a whole, these individual differences frequently are not as obvious because not everyone is required to contribute so much so continuously. But what happens to the students on both ends of the spectrum—the slow and unmotivated and the extremely bright? For the unmotivated students, the worst possibility is that they will get just as much by chance with this method as with any method. The more optimistic view is that their motivation will improve and the conditions will be flexible enough to allow them to perform and achieve more.

As for the bright students, the fear may be that they are too far ahead of their peers to gain anything from them. The activities of this program, however, are set up so that every day each person is responsible for some research, analysis, synthesis, and participation—not passive assimilation. Thus, the point of contention is not whether they get enough from their classmates; it is whether those so-called bright students are as yet sufficiently independent, self-motivated, and internally centered that they can accumulate and analyze their own information on a given topic. If they cannot, they have not truly learned. If one person is more gifted than others, he or she can still learn as much or more than before but with an added benefit—he or she can use that ability to share and teach. We have to teach everyone to share his or her abilities in teaching everyone else. Only then, by virtue of enough teachers, can we individualize and maximize diverse competencies that otherwise are wasted.

By thinking in terms of levels of knowledge inside individual minds, we tend to see people as containers to be molded and filled instead of as conduits to increase the amount and flow of information within a group. Knowledge should be cooperative and shared, not competitive and private. We should be trying to build a network of information that continues to grow, not simply a quantitive accumulation of smart individuals.

This structure maximizes the comprehension level of the class as a whole. The average level of task comprehension within any group is probably higher than the average of an entire class not divided into groups. In a group of thirty members, too many people become totally lost. They feel they cannot stop an entire class to ask questions—to do so would be too intimidating, impersonal, and embarrassing. Even if they did attempt to make a point, the sheer numbers of other students attempting to do the same would rule out significant follow-up on their idea as well as any further contributions from that person.

Small groups achieve just the opposite. Each person's contribution is significant, and the time between his or her contributions is potentially quite brief. In short, the sheer number of content-related ideas being generated within a class divided into groups is probably many times more than that generated in a thirty-person class. Certainly, on average, each student's individual contributions are also much greater. Not only are more ideas being generated, but also more are being shared, altered, and developed through reaction from group members. The ideas do not remain personal visions within one person's head that are then extinguished by lack of acknowledgment.

## Response in a Public Forum

Ideas must be expressed in a public forum to become meaningful. The teacher alone is not such a forum. Ideas must be exposed and held accountable to much probing: "I don't understand you." "What do you mean?" Ideas gain a life of their own only in public, where they are rethought and reexpressed, interact, grow, change, and die. When one has to explain an idea in public, one has to understand it, so each idea is thought through further than usual. This process is easily accomplished in groups.

For students, talking to peers is different from talking to a teacher-lecturer. Their psychological mind-set is immediately altered once it is apparent they are dealing with a grade-giving authority figure. Discussions in a teacher-dominated class are not really discussions at all. Verification or acknowledgment by the authority figure is the pivotal point around which the talk centers; all comments are funneled through this intermediary. Also, talk is organized around the teacher's expectations; the purpose is points, grades, or good impressions. Spectators look to the teacher for his or her reaction—facial, verbal, or body— which then determines their involvement or noninvolvement. Their personal, emotional, or intellectual reaction to a statement is first weighed, balanced, and rehearsed by imaginary projection through the teacher. This act of projection dulls, diverts, or kills the immediate response.

Part of the response process is grading, or evaluation, but in the proposed method most of it is done by the students themselves. Thus, much of the performing for the teacher's benefit is eliminated. As a result, through the use of student graders in different ways, the potential amount of meaningful, quality work that can be produced dwarfs anything that we have previously envisioned. Most teachers' usual practice of having to see every assignment severely limits the number of assignments they can make because they have only so much time for grading. Thus, students spend most of their time doing busy work until teachers finally get a batch of papers graded and can make another assignment. The teacher, not the student, is working all the time.

## Observations by Students

As mentioned earlier, some of the exercises require keeping

a journal. One question to be answered is, "What did you learn about learning today?" The students' answers and the ramifications of those answers are themselves rationale for this teaching method. Certain revelations keep appearing in the journals:
- shyness and loathing at the prospect of speaking to the group;
- a prior feeling that they are the only ones who think the way they do;
- a prior idea that other people think them stupid;
- a prior asumption that their thought world is private, weird, unique, not worth sharing, or superior;
- surprise that they can actually teach and that people listen to them and respect their ideas;
- the realization of how alike most students are;
- the realization that, in spite of all their fears and anxieties, they actually enjoyed speaking, enjoyed learning, and learned more in the groups.

The existence of so much self-doubt and fear points to the desperate need for these kinds of activities, and the resulting shifts in self-confidence, ability, and enjoyment point to their results and rewards.

The goal of these activities is to build on these new awarenesses. After all, such building should be the model of all learning, but usually teachers have no way of knowing what students are actually thinking and, thus, how to proceed. The journals provide student response.

Beyond these revelations about interactive learning, other opinions reflected in the journals are often inspiring—and yet, except for the journals, would not even be expressed. Each student in the class should be able to see other student's ideas and be inspired. These activities are designed for this purpose.

The ability to evaluate is an important critical thinking skill that is delegated to the students. The idea of students evaluating one another extends beyond grades and helps them learn to analyze incoming information so that they know what it is and understand it or know why they do not understand it. The student will learn to analyze and recognize the structure of information beyond the mere identification of a fact when it is presented. To be able to recognize how or why one is or is not stimulated, entertained, engrossed, and learning is an important step in realizing what is important in thinking. Evaluation exercises help students recognize organize, synthesize, and interpret information. The consequent sharing of the evaluation with the presenter creates an interchange of ideas between students that is immeasurably valuable.

## The Need for a Semester-long Commitment

Teachers are used to assuming—in fact, we take it as doctrine—that we are trying to develop independent, thinking, creative, and motivated self-learners. Consequently, if a new activity or approach fails to elicit behavior congruent with those goals, we simply dismiss the activity and return to more teacher-dominated activities. This sequence occurs over and over with all activities that stray too far and too often from the teacher-dominated classroom. Almost all teachers take refuge in these latter activities, as if to hide from the terrible secret to which they are now privy—that students are unable to behave in ways predicted by the goals—and in so doing, we perpetuate the social myth that schools help students attain the ultimate goals of education. For this reason we have dismissed all but one predominant teaching method—lecture, worksheets, and tests. The appallingly low levels of goal-related achievement and the paucity of variety of students' skills are not revealed in these methods because no skills—only memorization—are needed. The social myth remains intact because of misinterpretation and unconscious cover-up.

The broad outline of the teaching method presented thus far may have elicited snickers from skeptical readers. In chorus they predict that with this approach the students will do only the minimum of the work, misbehave, and not stay on the subject for more than half the period. Students, they say, need direction, reward, punishment, and forced feeding in order to learn.

Four responses immediately occur. First, all these criticisms concerning misbehavior, short attention spans, and low achievement also hold for traditional methods of teaching. The fact that the same difficulties may initially show up in these exercises should be no surprise.

Second, these criticisms assume that what is being learned must be the same as what traditional methods teach and must look as if traditional methods were used. That is, it must take the same amount of time, involve the same kind of efforts (papers, tests, and worksheets), and involve the exact same kind of content.

Third, these arguments assume that no other learning is occurring unless it takes the above apearance and if it does not, it is not as worthwhile as the traditional subject material.

Last, and most important, the problems and questions that may come to light as a result of trying these kinds of activities do not point to the pessimistic conclusions inherent in our usual methods—that students are unmotivated, lack the ability and desire for self-direction, and do not like to learn and thus must be forced to do so. Rather they present the converse message—that the schools have not taught or instilled motivation, self-direction, and joy of learning anywhere along the line. School-age students do not unselfconsciously exhibit these traits because the schools have not trained them to do so. Why do we teachers assume that if students are suddenly given an opportunity to display these traits in a high school activity, they will do so, if they have not practiced them before? And then, not having taught students these traits, why do we use their subsequent inabilities as justification to return to the old methods and continue not to teach these characteristics?

The irony is that if we look back to the curriculum or our lesson plans, the ultimate objective of our teaching is to develop self-directed, motivated learners. Our system sets up goals that are unattainable by the methods it proposes to use. And not only are they unattainable, but also the methods actually teach the opposite of those goals.

To summarize, any shortcomings in student performance in these activities indicate the fallacy not of this proposed method but of the one it supplanted, which made students unable to implement the new one. What has happened is that the locus of control has been removed from the student and relocated in the schools. That is why we teachers need to make a commitment to returning control of the learning process to the students. We need semester-long, year-long, and curriculum-wide commitments, not tentative dabbling. The exercises that follow are designed to reinforce this commitment. Used together, they can be the basis of a year-long format for teaching students to teach themselves.

**Part 2
How?**

# 4

# Overview of the Activities

The ideational and organizational foundations for the exercises that follow rest on the principles dicussed in part 1 Teachers must keep this in mind as they implement these or organize their own activities, because every facet of the activities is rooted in a multidimensional framework that transcends the content of a particular lesson. Each exercise should be seen only as a vehicle to the ends delineated in the first part. As such, the exercises are meant to provide a framework for teachers to create exercises to fit their own circumstances to students' ability levels, grade, or subject. The specifics of each activity can be altered to fit the teacher's needs: the number of days needed for certain exercises, the sources of student research and presentations, the combination of skills to be taught, the grading, the size of the groups, and so forth.

Developing activities to fulfill the goals of the first part can be a demanding chore. So many behaviors are desired that focusing on so many specific skills in each activity is difficult. One feature of this program works as your ally in this organization and helps keep you from getting lost in layers and layers of planning: every task of the activities requires a social and interactive performance that, by its multidimensional nature, brings to bear almost all the skills we would like to teach.

Consider the difference between how preschool children learn and how children and adolescents learn as they progress up the grade ladder. Physiological considerations aside, learning seems to slow down after early childhood—that is, after the learner is removed from an interactive relationship with his or her environment, where all the faculties are involved, and is told to learn only by listening. Restoring an interactive performance environment will create learning possibilities for many skills, whether or not you specifically target them in the activity.

A number of comments are necessary regarding the following activities. First, a point made in the introduction must be reiterated: although the activities were designed for high school social studies classes, the structure, procedures, and techniques can be used in all courses. Furthermore, the overall technique, not the individual pieces, is important.

Second, the titles of the exercises are somewhat arbitrary in that all the exercises teach most of the thinking skills referred to in the titles of the others. A title simply highlights the one or two skills or values that might be said to be the focus of that activity, whether the activity contains a specific skill lesson or that skill is the one most implicitly demanded by the activity's organization.

Third, the exercises are presented in no particular order because the basic structure of each is not course-specific and there is no inherent order. The specific requirements of each may be changed to fit the needs and abilities of a particular class.

Fourth, the activities assume at least rudimentary skills in many areas—reading, writing, speaking, and researching— but at the same time the exercises are designed to teach and allow practice of these skills. Complete mastery of these skills is not necessary for partipation in the exercises. If students cannot perform the requirements of the exercises at first, they soon will. The failures at the beginning of the activities simply become the lessons of following days. And these are lessons based on experiences that are visible to everyone at the same time. This mass experiential element is extremely instructive and leads to rapid improvement.

The activities should be arranged into a semester-long plan of progressive movement toward improving particular skills. In each activity, each skill is approached from a different direction and from a different level of accomplishment. Mastering most skills will take a number of activities, so each activity should demonstrate a higher level of accomplishment for that skill. In short, the complexity and level of performance will increase with each exercise as the students gain proficiency and become more acclimated to what they are doing.

Having a semester-long plan does not mean, however, that every day of the semester must be spent in group activities. Occasionally you will want to integrate full class periods into an activity, because they stress specific information that everyone must have, to teach the skills necessary to proceed with an activity, or to discuss the groups' progress or the lessons learned.

## Format of the Activities

Each activity divides up the responsibilities of the teacher and redistributes them among the students. The students, in turn, are divided into groups of 2-6 persons, each group then serving as a miniclass with all the roles and duties of teacher and students shared and exchanged within the group. Roles and responsibilities change periodically, both within a particular class period and from period to period and week to week. With this format the teacher is liberated from the minute-to-minute burden of creating and giving content-heavy lectures, period after period, day after day. With this freedom, the teacher can concentrate on the more multidimensional lessons that transcend content but do not neglect it. Following are some of these other lessons and how they can be included in every class period.

Typically, each exercise begins by presenting a handout to the students. This describes and explains the activity and is usually organized into several sections:

1. an introduction that orients the reader to the activity, explaining what it is and why it is relevant to the student;

2. a list of goals and skills that the activity is to accomplish or improve;

3. a skill lesson; and

4. a procedural section that gives the details of the activity. This will include every facet of procedure, including group membership, daily assignments, grading, topics, responsibility calendars, and operational mechanics.

This handout must be clear and comprehensive, for it is the operational guide to the activity, and both you and the students will need to refer to it continually. Explaining all the points of the guide may take an entire period or even longer if the activity is particularly complex or if it is the students' first excursion into this kind of group activity. Everyone must fully understand the organization; giving a quiz on it to make sure the handout is studied may be worthwhile.

## Fail-Safe Organization

In creating the activities, the teacher must make them as foolproof as possible, building in many fail-safe mechanisms. One goal must be to anticipate and block students' escape routes from doing the assignment (or, more accurately, escape routes from learning). These escape routes are well known; for example, everyone is familiar with reading worksheets, with their definitions of terms for the students to fill in. These are designed to make sure that reading is done; instead, the students look up the word in the index or in bold print and simply copy down the following sentence. This example can be multiplied many times over. For the teacher of a class of thirty or so students and as the sole grader of papers, however, this escape route is difficult to police.

In small groups, ensuring responsibility and performance is much easier. You have many "teachers" helping you, and you can require performance of every group member every day. The goal is to estabish an around-the-circle responsibility in which every person, every period, has a task. The ideal is to have every person contributing during every period for the entire period. Of course this is impossible, but you can program accountability for the whole period into these small groups. Students cannot hide behind anonymity in small groups.

Be prepared for any contingency. A group may simply break down, seek the lowest level of its collective ability, run out of things to do, or languish because the day's work rested too heavily on a person who did not come prepared. Several mechanisms, apart from the basic one of everyday responsibility for every person for the entire period, can be utilized in the exercises to prevent such a breakdown:

1. *Discussion questions.* One homework assignment of any activity can be requiring every person to formulate X number of discussion questions every day. These questions can be programmed into the activity as part of the assigned interaction for a day or as backup, with the following instructions: "If your group finishes with its assigned tasks for the day, then you will each ask your discussion questions, serving as both discussion leader and devil's advocate for that question. You will go around the group, each person asking one question at a time." To make sure that the students prepare these questions, even if they are not needed, someone in the group must be responsible for grading them.

2. *Group self-analysis.* If a group's activity comes to a stop, one good fail-safe mechanism is to have the group analyze its performance. Many students have difficulty with self-analysis. You may first have to teach them and provide sample questions to get them started. Group analysis is so valuable that it may be a required part of an activity, not simply a fail-safe backup feature. Getting students talking to one another about why they cannot talk to one another, fulfill the requirements, or act as a coherent group leads to awareness, problem solving, and self-correction that otherwise would not occur.

3. *Journals.* A similar backup tool is the journal. Its theme can be self-anaysis, group analysis, content analysis, or a combination. If the group discussion comes to an end, the students can write in their journals. Keeping a journal provides the

same kinds of thinking skills as those of group analysis, but writing skills, instead of speaking-social skills, are involved. For journals to work, however, someone in the group must record that they are being kept, or they must be handed in to the teacher periodically during the activity. The journals can also be included as part of the grade that the group gives itself or that the teacher gives the group. Whatever the method, some accountability has to be included.

Even if the students finish writing in the journals before the period is over, the group members can discuss their journal analyses. This kind of interrelatedness is what we must strive for: each facet of an exercise should be able to spawn another level of analysis.

4. *Group leaders*. Appointing group leaders can be effective also. These leaders can be awarded extra points for performing the duty of keeping the group moving on its intended path.

5. *Group dispersal*. If a group appears to have floundered beyond the point of any possible productive outcomes, you can split that group up for the rest of the period and send the members to other groups that are having more successful sessions. Not only are these students returned to a more active learning situation, but also they are exposed to more lively models, which they can try to emulate in future sessions.

6. *Teacher to the rescue*. You can always be waiting in the wings to jump in, if need be, to rescue the group from itself. You can take over the student-teacher's duties for the rest of the period. In fact, you may want to schedule yourself into different groups on different days to act as both teacher and role model for group discussion facilitator. On such days, you can appoint a student observer to watch over all the groups and evaluate all the teachers (including yourself, of course).

7. *Minimum time requirements for the group teacher's presentation*. At first, you may have to require a minimum time to qualify for certain grades ("A" = 45 minutes, "B" = 40 minutes,

"C" = 35 minutes). This is not an arbitrary time requirement, although it looks like one. It forces students to explore their subject more deeply and from more angles. Typically, students tend to stop thinking at or just below the surface of a topic. They stop just beyond the obvious or after they have retrieved the minimum required information. They do not then dissect and examine that information. They do not play with it, manipulate it, or extrapolate from it. They do not make value judgments or try to imagine the impact in differing situations. The time requirement will force them to do all of these.

The goal of each of these fail-safe mechanisms must be to make each into a skill-practicing activity, not simply a time filler. The organizational ideal is to structure an activity that has fail-safe mechanisms but does not need them. To this end, it is important continually to monitor group performance. At the beginning of each period you may want to devote a few minutes to discussing any problems you noticed the previous day. At first it is difficult for students to learn from previous days' mistakes unless you help. Students might criticize or be bored by another student's presentation but then go on to make the same mistakes. They take this approach because it is safest and easiest. To prevent this, you should discuss the strengths and weaknesses of the presentations and performances of each group member and focus on how they might be improved. Requiring the students to fill out a personal improvement chart after each presentation will help. This chart is a self-examination based on the student's own experience, peer evaluation, and the teacher's evaluation.

The teacher's role as observer is important for the efficient functioning of the activities. As you sit outside the groups (it is best to sit where you can see and hear all of them, not hover over any one group), you will see new and different problems occur every day. You must resist coming immediately to the rescue; instead, observing how the group handles a problem can be interesting and instructive. You should mention the problem at the beginning of the next class, however.

Because the role of observer is so important and also so instructive, students should also play that role. Every day a different student can observe and then report his or her findings to the class the next day.

# Group Dynamics

The successful design of a fail-safe activity depends partly on how the teacher organizes the groups. Every activity involves groups in some manner, so when you are putting them together, be sure to consider several questions:

- What kind of group is it to be? What is its function?
- How small can a group be and remain effective? How large?
- What are the different ways of picking groups? Factors to consider are free choice, ability levels, behavior, friendships, continuous absentees, attitudes, personalities, and random assignment.
- How long should you keep any combination of students together in a group? How can you tell when it is time to change group members? The time for change will vary from class to class; you will have to play it by ear and have a ready system to reshuffle groups. Having the same group work together for up to two weeks can be quite effective. However, a group, like water, seeks it lowest level, and until students become adept at this type of learning, finding that level may take several days. If the lowest level is quite high, however, then there is no problem. If not, reshuffling might be the answer. New faces are positive stimuli, not fear-inducing ones. Often what spurs discussion is not becoming comfortable with a group but uncertainty and the lack of set expectations or pecking order.
- How many groups can operate in a class without becoming too noisy? I have found 5-6 groups do not make too much noise. In fact, a little noise is actually advantageous. The constant buzz in the background makes each group feel as if it is not alone on center stage.
- How long should the particular structure and content of a group's responsibility be maintained? Recognizing when to

change structure and content stimuli is important. Just as a lecture can become monotonous, so can the structure and content of a group discussion.

Once you get the groups together, you will find that they may each develop their own personality:

- problem solvers
- note-taking listeners
- animated discussers
- unruly
- uninterested
- interested, serious, and sincere
- task oriented
- zany and loud
- quiet, shy, less emotional
- personal, intimate, and concerned
- dead.

In short, a small group allows an active chemistry to form between group members. This chemistry cannot be anticipated or avoided. Suppressing these personalities and forcing them all into one "ideal" type is a common mistake; this approach will not work and will actually suppress the group's developed learning style. As you shuffle group membership, everyone will be exposed to different kinds of groups.

Two kinds of groups should be of concern, however. The first is the dead or dying group. Some groups, for whatever reason, simply lose their life. If simple prodding or motivation does not work, then perhaps you will have to divide, reorganize, split, or recombine that group. If shuffling is not practical, you might want to redefine the group's task so that it will be more amenable to its personality. Ideally, however, your organization of the activity will have enough built-in mechanisms so that it can compensate for a complete breakdown on a given day within any given group.

The second kind of group that might be of concern is the misbehaving group. Again, prevention built into the structure is the best answer, but there is another less obvious and perhaps more important answer. A behavior's disruptive consequence depends on the situation. In a small group, behaviors that cannot be allowed during a classwide lecture may be perfectly acceptable. The groups will experience "down times" and will misbehave at times, but the students will return to the task relieved and at ease. A minute break revitalizes them and does not disrupt the class as a whole.

# Common Procedural Features of the Activities

Each suggested activity entails many skills and duties. The skills are multidimensional in that they require many kinds of thoughts, behaviors, and products. Furthermore, these behaviors and products are called upon continuously and much more frequently than is possible in most other class situations. (A summary of the common structures of the upcoming activities follows.) The important point to remember is that these skills are performed by almost everybody every day in one form or another.

*Speaking*

Speaking responsibilities may range from five minutes every day to fifty minutes two days in a row. Within that range are many combinations: ten minutes every day, two minutes five times a day, thirty minutes every fifth day and 5-10 minutes every day in between, and so forth.

The size of the audience can vary also. A student may be speaking to two people or to the entire class. Most typically, however, the audience is composed of about five other students.

The kind of speaking also varies. One day a student might be a teacher, the next a questioner, and the next a so-called minipresenter, responsible for a five-minute report.

*Writing*

Again, many combinations of writing responsibilities are possible. Every student may write every night for ten minutes, every three days for an entire period for three weeks, or every night for a half hour; other combinations are also possible. All these assignments can produce huge amounts of writing that no teacher could ever hope to grade, evaluate, and comment on, but since the group miniclasses consist of only six persons on average, each with six teachers, the processing, grading, and learning from this massive volume of writing are relatively easy. Selected pieces will still come across your desk, and you will occasionally grade the students' evaluations of one another. This process results in continual practice and evaluation, which in turn leads to the teacher's increased ability to diagnose writing problems more accurately, focus on those problems, and develop assignment activities as prescriptive remedies.

*Listening*

Students are supposed to be listening all the time, but in large classes there is no real need to do so. In these small groups, every student will have to respond several times during a period to what has just been discussed; thus, students will pay attention so as not to look silly. Also, in a large class, not listening and looking silly a couple of times is worth the risk because the teacher inevitably stops calling on that student, who will then be free to daydream for the rest of the semester. Furthermore, in a larger class, whether the student answers a teacher's question will not have any effect on the class or its proceedings—the teacher will just keep talking.

But in small groups each student has an assigned role on which every other role is partly dependent. If the student does not fulfill his or her role, this failure hurts everyone else. Thus, the tendency is to try much harder, no matter how poor a student a person might be.

*Reading*

Again, each homework assignment will involve varying amounts of reading, depending on what the student's role is the next day. Some students may be reading as research for a teaching role, some to answer questions that the teacher asked them to research, and some to take a quiz on the reading. The reading texts may vary also. Some students will be reading magazines, some textbooks, and some supplemental books.

This structure of reading for different purposes and different roles every day gives an added meaning and urgency to the reading. Each student is required to do something with that reading every day and to do it in public. This factor is not only a powerful incentive; it also increases students' interest in the reading.

### Introspection

Many of the activities have parts that involve self- or group analysis. As mentioned before, this analysis is both oral and written and occurs daily, weekly, or as one comprehensive session at the end of the activity. The chapter on introspective thinking (exercise 5) contains a good example of a framework in which the group is required to analyze its own performance. Other exercises require students to keep a journal of their own thoughts on the content, the group, their performance, learning, and teaching. This sort of self-assessment, coupled with the evaluations of others, leads to improvement.

### Grades

The frequency and sources of grades also have their own spectrum. At least one performance is evaluated every day, but sometimes as many as three or four grades come from different sources every day. Students may grade themselves or be graded by each of their peers in their group, by all the students in the class, by a group leader, or by the teacher. In addition, there may be group grades—grades that a group may give itself, that the class may give itself, or that the teacher may give to each group or to the class as a whole. There may even be cooperative grades, in which everyone in a group gets the same grade or every group in the class gets the same grade. On a given day, any combination of these grades is possible.

The performances that are graded vary also. A student may be graded for only one kind of performance during a period or for three, four, or five performances. These grades may be for teaching, minipresentations, two-minute analyses, questions, essays, evaluations, effort, contributions, or teamwork. With so many teachers, so few students, and so many helpers, the amount of response and evaluation possible is much greater than with almost any other method.

### Skill Lessons

Every activity is designed primarily to teach and develop various thinking skills. In fact, in creating an exercise, the teacher must always be thinking of ways to elicit the desired behaviors and thinking style. The structure of the activity is centered around these behaviors, and the particular content is simply used as raw material for practicing these skills. If all the skills are effectively brought into play, not only is the content more effectively learned but also one's ability to learn is improved. This process is self-reinforcing, for all learning thereafter accelerates and deepens.

Do not make the mistake of organizing any social situation and then saying, "I taught them social interaction." Just doing something does not teach unless the learners are aware of what they are doing, are actively engaged in analyzing how they are learning, and are observing the changing appearance of this learning. A guide must be constantly present; this guide might be the teacher, an element built into the daily activities of the exercise (like the journals, which allow the students to analyze the group performance and their relation to and ideas about it), or the students themselves, by requiring them to discuss their performances and what they see happening.

In fact, integrating the thinking skill lessons into the activity is the most truly interactive way to provide these lessons. Perhaps you can schedule a "lesson day" every two, three, or four days or half a period every two days. These lessons will focus on the desired skill and use examples—good and bad—from all the activities. This approach grounds everything you teach in actual experience. Students recognize it, feel it, and often personally relate to it.

You cannot give a lesson or organize activities for every skill that may be required in any given activity. The important point is that, to some degree, all skills are required in continuously participatory and social settings allowing response, learning, and change. Further, each skill must be called forth in conjunction with many other complementary skills so that learning takes place in a holistic environment. As long as all faculties are open, all can be improved, even though only one may be dominant at one time. In our usual lecture mode, without participation and response, all faculties except listening and memory are closed.

The elements common to all the activities—speaking, writing, listening, reading, introspection, grades, and skill lessons—should be kept in mind while studying the following chapters, each of which represents one exercise. Keeping these elements in mind will help you as the teacher internalize the basic blueprint of the activities and better enable you to decipher the purpose and efficacy of any particular feature or the quality of an activity as a whole. Furthermore, keeping the big picture in mind will better enable you to observe shortcomings, devise alternatives, foresee problems, and create your own activities. These activities are merely a framework of procedural ideas you can build, integrate, or delete to meet your own needs.

The remaining chapters of the second part each present a different activity. The presentation of these activities is directed toward teachers, but the format is essentially that of a handout for the students regarding the particular activity.

The first activity is the most complete in that it opens with a summary lesson of the main skill—questioning skills—to be achieved once the activity is underway. The other activities shorten this presentation to the procedure of an activity, and a chosen skill lesson is assumed to precede or be integrated into that activity. The particular skill can be one of many since each activity involves so many. For each activity, I have indicated which of the many skills involved may be considered the main focus of the activity and thus of the lesson. Others could be chosen. You will notice that the targeted skills are always above and beyond the subject matter of the course. The idea is always to use the subject matter as a catalyst to attain much broader skills, which, in turn, facilitate and increase the learning of the subject matter.

Virtually every part of every activity can branch out into a new lesson or open the door to the development of new activities. The branching is interminable, and the possible directions for future classes become almost overwhelming. As a result, at every juncture questions will well up in your mind: "What should I do here?" "Give an example of how this can be developed." Except in some cases, the answers must be determined by the reader. The process of creation-question-creation snowballs. As the activities begin to unfold in class, you learn right along with the students. The observations about teaching, learning, and thinking become a continuous stream. You approach every day full of excitement, not only for what the students are doing but also for what you might observe and learn.

**5**

# Exercise 1:
# Learning
# By Questioning

This activity is designed to teach students how to learn by asking questions. The idea for this approach grew out of a desire to stimulate curiosity and thinking beyond the boundary of memorization. Students have great difficulty formulating questions to be used as the basis for discussion. Usually their questions range from "What is such and such?" to "What do you think about such and such?" This difficulty is indicative of an inability to step back from a topic and see its relation and relevance to other ideas. It is also indicative of a lack of practice in abstracting, analyzing, comparing, extrapolating, and combining ideas—all functions that require a holistic and integrative relationship with a topic. Most students view the world of ideas as composed of unrelated bits and pieces instead of a seamless, flowing continuum.

What better way to start practicing these skills than by requiring all learning to take place by asking questions? The teaching method proposed here helps students recognize how different aspects of a topic are   related to one another, how to recognize the parts of a complex idea and how they fit together, how an idea can be extended beyond itself, how an idea can be related to other ideas, and how the implications of an idea may have relevance to their lives. This exercise teaches how to approach and analyze a subject (with different levels of questions aimed at different results), gives hundreds of examples, and provides an opportunity for continual and intensive practice. Thus, its purpose is to enhance and expand the students' natural curiosity, not straitjacket it with the attitude that there is only one outcome—"correct" answers.

The content of this activity as presented here is for a tenth-grade course entitled "Western Man."

# Introduction for Students: History as a Reflection of Ourselves

History is not extraneous to life, as students often think—people live it! They often think of historical characters as book characters; they each have their chapter or unit but not real lives. Sometimes students are surprised when a character re-emerges after the unit is over. Usually he or she reappears only as a supporting character, and they think of him or her in terms of the new unit; characters' "history lives" are only so many pages long.

This is sterile thinking. Human beings think and feel and create history. Movies such as "Reds," "Gallipoli," "Amadeus," and "The Killing Fields" help bring this idea home to the students. They must be trained to see that the events they are studying are not mere tales recorded in textbooks; rather, they actually happened to people. History is their reactions, emotions, and ideas in certain circumstances.

If we assume that through the centuries human beings have remained basically the same, then history is the study of our reactions to and emotions and ideas about these circumstances. Furthermore, reactions to circumstances in history are to a certain extent reflections of ourselves. History brings into focus the stuff of which we are made. Revealed throughout history is humankind's spirit, intelligence, humor, and compassion—all our good points. But also revealed are our hatred, aggression, brutality, and stupidity—all our shortcomings. These high points and low points are the essence of history and its meaning. The events are simply the frame on which we hang the phenomenon of humankind. Textbooks depict the frame only; thus, students are not made aware of the human aspects of history when they read them, and they have difficulty seeing themselves in history. Thus, when reading history in this form, they have to read with their whole selves, not just with the test-taking, fact-memorizing part of themselves.

This activity is an attempt to look at history in ways that broaden its meaning, relevance, and interest. The main strategy is to teach students how to ask questions in order to lead them into more fruitful, expansive, and interesting areas of thought. The object is to have students look inside themselves and identify those elements of our humanity that have played the most significant roles in history.

## Assumptions, Goals, and Skills

This activity is based on several assumptions:
- Everyone wants to learn;
- Learning is a skill that must be developed;
- People learn best when given a specific task but allowed flexibility in the performance of that task;
- People must take responsibility for their own learning;
- People learn best by participating actively in their learning.
- Students are the main resource in a classroom. Students are as smart as the teacher, on average, and there are thirty times as many. Thus, the interaction of thirty brains will produce many more thoughts than one brain acting singly, and the consequent learning will be much greater than otherwise possible;
- Cooperation is more productive and humane than competition.

This activity has the following goals:
- to teach students questioning skills,
- to allow practice of outlining skills,
- to allow practice of speaking skills,
- to allow practice of social and communication skills,
- to teach the value of cooperation versus competition,
- to show history from many viewpoints,
- to allow practice of organizational skills;
- to teach students to learn with their entire being, not just their minds,

- to teach the facts of history,
- to teach students to analyze group dynamics,
- to teach students to analyze the learning process,
- to teach students to examine their own beliefs and abilities, and
- to build self-confidence.

Start with an explanation of the assumptions, goals, and skills because they frame the activity for the students. Usually teachers' plans do not let the students in on what exactly we are "doing for them." Thus, they never see the reason, context, or value of the work, and consequently, they do not learn what they are "supposed" to learn. This activity has many goals; some are directly aimed at, others only indirectly. All the assumptions and goals are part of the lesson and should be discussed at length.

Most of the assumptions, goals, and skills referred to in the exercises are similar, but each activity has one or two unique goals that are of major value for that particular activity. Even where the assumptions and goals are similar, each activity places different emphasis on different ones. Remember that the skills cannot be fully learned in one exercise; they must be continually practiced in as many contexts and situations as possible to ensure a more rounded development.

## Learning Is Questioning

The following material represents the outline of a lesson on how to learn by asking questions (the organization and procedure of the activity itself follows this lesson). This outline can be written into the student handout or can be taught at any time or any point in any activity. Some activities have two or three skills that could be taught at two or three points.

Determining whether actively to teach a skill depends on whether it is absolutely necessary for the functioning of the activity or whether it is peripheral and can be learned by assimilation and experience as the activity progresses. Another determinant is whether you have planned a comprehensive lesson on that skill in another activity. Instead of having one in-depth lesson, you may want to have shorter, more frequent lessons for particular skills throughout all the activities or combine them with an in-depth one. These latter two choices are the most attractive because every skill is progressively learned and will need ever more practice and ever more conceptual input to push it to the next stage of accomplishment. Questioning skills, for example, are employed in every activity of this teaching program; follow-up and advancement in these skills should therefore continue after the present activity, and the successes and failures of each activity can serve as raw material and examples for future lessons. This progressiveness is important if the lessons are to fulfill their potential.

Inserting all these skill lessons into the activities is beyond the scope of this book. The possibilities are virtually limitless; they depend on the needs and goals of a particular class.

Asking questions is one of the most important aspects of understanding information. In order to ask a complex question, the brain must go through many processes:

1. It must comprehend the basic facts;

2. It steps back and sees how those facts fit in with what else you know;

3. It assesses the relationship between known and unknown and postulates a relationship that requires verification;

4. It must recognize what is important or relevant; thus, it is always associating and taking apart information;

5. It takes information apart to analyze cause and effect and seeks verification;

6. It combines separate bits of information to form a larger whole and seeks reinforcement.

Asking questions is a constant taking apart, putting back together, and reshuffling into new creations. At their highest level, questions probe, discover, explore, and manipulate information. They constantly seek new and stable ways to understand information.

Questions force students to look further, dig deeper, and, at times, change their thinking altogether. Questions force them to check their assumptions and expand the horizons of their mind's vision. Without any further acquisition of facts, they can take and use those facts to build a world of thought many times larger than the one with which each student started.

## Devising Discussion Questions

Formulating penetrating questions is not always an easy task. It requires practice. When asked to make up some discussion questions, students who had not had any practice gave examples such as this one:

*Question*—What are "belligerents"? *Answer*—Warring nations. Is an opinion expressed here? No. Does the answer have two sides to it? No. Does the answer encompass complicated concepts? No. It is simply a definition. Students have to know definitions in order for any further thinking to take place, but the goal is to learn these so they can get to more intriguing thoughts.

How was this example formulated? The reader probably looked for a bold print word, put "What is?" in front of it, and proclaimed it a discussion question. This is not the way to formulate a discussion question.

Is it worthwhile as a discussion question? A good way to determine whether your question has any value is to ask these questions: So what? Does it matter? Does the answer have a meaning for history and humankind? If it does have meaning, does the wording of the question get to it?

If a student wanted to use "belligerents" in a question, he or she would have to frame the question to give the word more meaning:

"Belligerents" means warring nations. What moral principles justify one nation's attempt to war against another nation? Is war immoral or illegal? Explain. If either, how is it possible for a government to force it on its own people? How is it possible that a government can say it is illegal to kill people but at the same time demand that you do so if you are at war?

The answers to these kinds of questions do matter. These questions were made by taking a concept and turning it around in one's mind, viewing it from different perspectives, and relating it to to other ideas.

The process can be implemented in many ways. One way is Bloom's hierarchy.[1] Bloom classifies six types of thinking, each of which is "higher" than the next. Below is a chart of these categories, the kind of knowledge each represents, and some key words that, when used in a question, will get at that category of knowledge:

| Category | Kind of Knowledge | Key Words |
|---|---|---|
| Knowledge | recalling, remembering | who, what, where, when, locate, identify, match |
| Comprehension | understanding, ability to state in own words | give example, summarize, infer, explain |
| Application | ability to apply to new situations and real life | organize, experiment, predict what would happen if. . . |
| Analysis | separating into parts, finding similarities and differences | identify, distinguish, compare, contrast; What is the premise of. . . What is the function of. . . What is the relationship between . . . |
| Synthesis | combining bits of information | make, add to, combine suppose, hypothesize |
| Evaluation | making a judgment or decision as to something's rightness, wrongness, or worth and defending that judgment | justify, criticize, judge, solve, recommend |

By using these key words, students can direct their questions into higher and higher orders of thinking. Note, however, that all levels of thinking require knowledge and comprehension as the foundations of thinking.

Another way to generate questions is to take a sentence and dissect it. What are its elements? Students may find many ways to put this sentence back together and relate its elements to other ideas in order to formulate new relationships:

- One question may generate another question;
- An answer may generate a question;
- The past can be related to the present;
- The general can be related to the specific;
- The personal can be related to the public;
- The emotional can be related to the intellectual;
- Experience can be related to imagination.

The following is an example of question brainstorming that uses many of these techniques. All the questions that follow were generated by reading the following three sentences:

> In the early 1900s many people believed that the world was on the verge of a long era of prosperity and peace. They thought that scientific and industrial progress would create a better life than anyone had ever known. They believed that widespread education would prepare people to govern themselves with wisdom and moderation.

The questions that derive from this passage include:

1. What events and ideas in the recent past made people at the turn of the century believe that a long era of peace and prosperity lay ahead?

2. Give specific examples.

3. Were they right? Why or why not?

4. What was it about the scientific, industrial, or education revolution that made people optimistic?

5. What change in events and thinking made circumstances different?

6. How are ideas important in shaping events?

7. What is the dominating idea of American society today?

8. What is the mood of our country?

9. When the history of our time is written, what will the introductory sentence be? "When humankind entered the 1980s, there was only one concern—will there be a tomorrow? Will there be a 1990s?" Or: "Mankind moved into the 1980s at the speed of light, or nearly so, for it seemed that high technology would make everything possible—including actual travel at the speed of light."

10. What warning signs pointed to the fallacy of this assumption of peace and prosperity?

11. Why were they not taken seriously?

12. If today we can see the many causes of World War I, why could not the people then see them and prevent it?

13. If hindsight is 20/20, is present sight blind? Why or why not?

If this number of questions can be created (and thirteen is a fraction of the number that can be generated) from three sentences, imagine how much information and how many ideas students will be able to find locked up or hidden within an entire chapter. Each sentence points beyond itself into an entire universe of ideas. Surely, everyone can find a home in one of those universes.

## Historically Relevant Questions: A List

The list that follows is simply a list of historically oriented questions that resulted from a brainstorming session and could be asked about any chapter in general. These questions are to be used as guides for the students in formulating their own questions and to demonstrate the kind of issues and concepts that lie hidden beneath each sentence. The sentences should serve as triggers that release these questions.

1. Is war simply a continuation of politics by other means?

2. What justifies war?

3. Has the nature of war changed from previous times to today? How?

4. Have the reasons for war changed?

5. Are these reasons better, worse, or the same as those before?

6. Is force the ultimate answer in human affairs?

7. Does might make right?

8. Could a history book be written depicting only events of love, goodness, and aid among people? Could history be interpreted in this light?

9. Politics seem to predominate in history. Why is this?

10. Are the important events in your assignment political? If not, how would you describe them?

11. What is it about political events that makes them so important to society? Why for example, do they make the front page of the newspaper while the comics or sports section does not?

12. What are the most important political events or trends in our country and the world today?

13. Compare the nature of the events today with the nature of earlier events. Are the concerns and issues basically the same as those of today, or are they different?

14. What kind of person would you have to be to influence history?

15. If you were this person, what would you try to influence and how?

16. What factors would influence your choices?

17. What or who would be in your way?

18. Looking around the classroom, can you imagine that anyone here might influence the course of history?

19. Who determines whether someone's or some event's influence on history is good or bad? Can some influence be seen both ways?

20. When we read history textbooks, the past seems full of such earth-shaking events, action, immediacy, urgency, and importance. Soon our time is going to be past. Do you feel history happening around you? Do you feel important, as if at the crest of some wave of historical significance? Does history as presented in texts leave out the everyday life in which the great events are immersed?

21. Are events happening around the world important to you?

22. Are you aware of world trends or directions today?

23. Do you think the masses of people of past eras were aware of the trends of their day?

24. Do you think most people today are informed about their world? More informed than people of the past?

25. Do you think it makes a difference in the course of events if the public knows what is going on or not?

26. Is the world better today than in the past?

27. This course is history as seen through Western eyes. Try to view history through the eyes of an African or Chinese person. Whose view is right? Are we right because we are Americans and the most powerful nation on earth? Are we the most power nation because we are right? If we are right, why does not everyone else in the world want to be just like us?

28. What are the differences between industrial, scientific, and political revolutions? How are they similar? Does your assignment cover any revolutions?

29. Why does a revolution of any sort happen? What are the causes? Are its effects noticeable as it is occurring? Can it be gradual and unnoticed? Are some easier to see in retrospect? Is any kind of revolution going on in our country or the world right now?

30. What is the role of modernization in the history of the world? What problems does it solve? What problems does it create?

31. How has technology changed the world and the pace of history?

32. Who runs the world—humans or machines?

33. How has the machine changed humankind's work, leisure, philosophy, religion, and relationship with the earth?

34. If new solutions bring new problems, is there such thing as progress?

35. Is the quality of life improving for the world as a whole? If so, is it improving fast enough?

36. How do you measure "quality of life"? Is it better now than 200 years ago? Do you think people who lived 200 years ago would agree with you if they visited us now?

37. Have we learned from our mistakes, or do we constantly seem to be making the same mistakes over and over? If you think we don't learn, why is this and what does it mean for the future of humankind? If you think we do learn, do you envision some sort of perfect society in the future?

38. Can the nations of the world become closer through cooperation?

39. Are the world's differences just political, economic, or cultural? Are there other kinds of differences?

40. Is there a basic drive in human nature that prevents the world's nations from cooperating for the benefit of all? Are these drives the driving forces of history?

41. Do you feel in control of your destiny?

42. How did people in the past feel about free will versus determinism? Why?

43. How much control do you have over history? More than people in the past? Less?

44. Is conflict a necessary or inevitable part of human relations? Of international relations?

45. Civilizations have risen and fallen. New ones have thriven where old ones died. Why is this?

46. What signs do you see in the world today of rising and falling civilizations? Give examples and reasons. Are the reasons the same for the rise and fall of past civilizations? Can you make any generalizations? Does each age produce its own unique conditions for such rising and falling?

47. What signs do you see in your assigned text as to whether the country you are studying is rising or falling?

48. What is the proper size of nations?

49. Why do countries strive for giganticism? Why did the U.S. seek Manifest Destiny? What other examples of expansionism can you point to in history? Are nations still trying to expand today? Can anyone in any time succeed? What were the limiting

factors in your assigned period of history? What are the limiting factors today?

50. Are history and time the same? What is the difference? How are they connected?

51. Why is history always being revised? How can it be revised if what happened really happened?

52. What is the relationship between ideals and reality? Is there any separation between the two? Trace any difference between the two in your assignment. Are our ideals today the same or different from the ideals of earlier historical periods?

53. What forces do you feel impinge on your freedom? Why do you suppose these forces are so powerful? Have they been built up for many years? Are these the same forces that people felt in the past? How did they become so powerful? Can they be changed?

54. So much history has occurred. Are we here today because every event in history combined to create the exact circumstances that produced each of us?

55. If one thing happened differently in 1800—if Napoleon had slept late one day, for example—would that have changed the history of the world? Would it have affected whether you or I were born?

56. What is the role of the military power in government? Why do people tolerate it? Is it necessary? If so, why? Has it always been necessary? Will it always be necessary?

57. What events do we choose to look at as history? Why these?

58. What are the events that made history? Were they considered good or bad by the dominant mode of thought of society at that time? From our knowledge of the consequences, were they good or bad?

59. Do different cultures represent different ways of thinking? If so, how do we account for this when we are involved in world politics? Would we devise different solutions to world problems if we saw the world through others' eyes? Are United States solutions better? Should we shape the world in America's image?

60. What do you think about the concept of world government? Would it have helped prevent World War I, World War II, or the war in Vietnam?

61. Which governments do you think are best able to solve the pressing problems of their own nation and the world? Why? Are certain kinds of governments better at solving problems than others? Has this been true throughout history?

62. Are there now or have there ever been any real instances of the people of a nation wielding power? What does "power to the people" mean? How can it be implemented?

63. Why do certain conditions produce certain kinds of governments?

64. Looking at the rise and fall of nations throughout history, how long do you think the United States will remain the most powerful? Do you think nation's reigns are longer or shorter in the modern world than in the past?

65. Which is more powerful—ideas or weapons? Has this been true throughout all ages?

66. What is more powerful—love or hate?

Each one of these questions could be used as the trunk of a branching question tree. As such, perhaps some of them will help students formulate their own questions in the following activity.

# Organization

Most of the activities are fairly complicated and, in the beginning, may take an entire period or even two to set up. At first, while you are explaining the orgaization, the students may be confused. For these reasons, it is better to use shorter exercises at first and then move on to longer ones. Students will become quite good at the format as they use it again and again.

The class will be divided into a number of groups (3-6 persons, depending on class size). The number of people to include in a group is subject to many considerations. The exercise itself can accommodate many combinations, so the primary consideration is the optimum number for ensuring maximum participation while simultaneously accomplishing the greatest quantity and highest quality of work. With too few students, the number of tasks that can be divided among them diminishes or else the burden increases beyond their ability to perform. Also, the fewer the students, the greater the chance that the group will fail. Too much responsibility will be resting on the shoulders of too few, and one student's poor performance or lack of effort will have a proportionately greater effect on the group.

On the other hand, if a group is too big, each student's degree of participation will decline. Although a greater quantity and variety of tasks can be divided among the members, the quality and breadth of participation and learning will be diluted.

Each group will be assigned a chapter of the text, and students within that group will teach and train one another on that chapter. The assignment does not have to be a chapter of a textbook, although this is convenient; it can be any learning unit whatsoever. Depending on the size of the unit, different skills will be elicited. An assignment requiring presentations of an entire chapter in two days, for example, might place a great premium on summary skills, the ability to extract the main points, and the ability to see the big picture. If units are smaller or spread out over more time, the emphasis may be on more details, facts, and anlyses.

On assigned dates, the members of a group will individually teach one of the other groups the chapter on which they have become experts; for example, on March 22, the group assigned chapter 17 will teach the other groups that chapter. These reports to the other groups will last for two days. The number of days for a presentation, as with any exercise in this book, can be altered, as, consequently, can the length of any exercise.

Each student in the class has an assignment and a presentation every day. These daily presentations require constant vigilance. If some students are still not participating, you can alter some of the rules or the organization as you go. Adaptation is relatively easy because in this teaching approach you can think in terms of classes of six persons. The possibilities for eliciting participation when you have to think only in terms of organizing the activities of a few students are endless. The complexity of orchestrating interaction is thus greatly reduced while the possibilities greatly increase.

All grades are cooperative. Each student's grade depends not only on his or her own effort and performance but also on every other student's effort. Cooperative grading can be tricky, and a great deal of judgment is necessary. You probably will have to set individual goals for individual students. Look for evidence of risking, trying, and improving—anything that in any way displays self-transcending activity. You may have to let certain poor or rebellious students have a free ride on the performance of better students. Or you may have to let better students be dragged down somewhat. You could give cooperative grades for only some parts of the exercise; thus, each student would get his or her own grade, which would be either helped or hindered to a certain degree by the cooperative efforts of the group or class. Also, you might have to make the exception that a student who does a poor job can flunk even if the class does not or that a student who does a great job cannot flunk, even if the group does.

You will have to give a group grade every day so that the students can get a feel for what is expected; they need critiquing. But you will also have to raise the standards and expectations of performance for grades as the activity progresses. In short, creating a cooperative situation without at the same time diluting the value of that cooperation is tricky.

### Phase I: Intragroup Teaching (four days)

The members of each group will teach one another the chapter for which their group is responsible. Once they are "experts" on their own chapter (in this case, after four days), the second phase begins: the members will all go to the other groups to teach everyone else the chapter. If for some reason there are more groups than teachers, split the members of the extra groups among those with teachers. After this presentation (two days), the teaching group will reunite. A different group will then split up and teach their chapter to the other groups.

*Groups*. Each chapter group will meet for four days to teach one another and to prepare a presentation to give to the other groups. The first three days will be devoted to intensive intra-group teaching. The fourth day will be spent putting all material together into a presentation to give to the other groups. A portion of each day will be devoted to compiling, as a group, a list of 30-50 questions that will be part of each of the individual presentations to the other groups.

Your role during these four days, as in all the activities, will be to orchestrate all this activity. Reminders of what will be happening today, tomorrow, and the next day must be given, and you will constantly need to reframe what has happened thus far into he context of what is going to happen.

*Roles and Rotation.* You will divide group responsibilities for the intragroup teaching into the following categories: teacher, philosopher, time traveler, questioner, and summarizer. These responsibilities will be assigned by a format similar to the following rotating schedule:

## Roles

| Name | Day 1 | Day 2 | Day 3 |
|------|-------|-------|-------|
| Joe | teacher | questioner | philosopher |
| Bill | teacher | summarizer | time traveler |
| Mary | philosopher | teacher | questioner |
| Frank | time traveler | teacher | summarizer |
| Pete | questioner | philosopher | teacher |
| Sue | summarizer | time traveler | teacher |

Obviously, these roles can be valuable in stimulating students to think in different ways, but you may find it necessary to give lessons on how to think in each of these ways.

■ *Teacher*—At the first meeting the teacher will divide the sections of the chapter equally among the group members. This section is what each student will teach on the day that he or she is the teacher.

Each person will teach his or her section(s) to the group. According to the previous example, Joe and Bill will teach on the first day, Mary and Frank the second day, and Sue and Pete the third day.

The teacher's main responsibility is to make sure that everyone knows the facts of the chapter—who, what, where, and so forth.

■ *Philosopher*—When it is a student's turn to be the philosopher, he or she will examine, study, think about, and present the philosophical implications of his or her section to the group. The philosopher's task is to examine the information of the section and take it beyond the chapter. He or she will be required to ask many questions that relate the information to human nature, world problems, the nature of society, the nature of government, the nature of progress, reasons for hope and despair, and so forth. Some of the questions in the questions list will provide hints, but the philosopher should formulate his or her own, derived from the specific information in the chapter.

■ *Time traveler*—The time traveler's job is to relate the past to the present. What events and ideas of the assigned period seem to influence events and ideas of today? How does the past influence the present? Have we learned from our mistakes? Are some of our ideas today attempts to behave and think differently from in the past? Why did they believe differently then?

Also, the time travelers must try to relate to the life and times of the age they are studying. They are to try to bring these people to life, make them real, and appeal to students' emotions and intuition in showing what it would be like to live in those times and under those circumstances.

■ *Questioner*—This person is to think up as many meaningful discussion questions as possible. They can relate to any aspect of the sections for which he or she is responsible as well as all possible types of relationships of subject matter. With these questions he or she is to dissect, synthesize, create, evaluate, judge, and analyze the chapter and its ramifications for history. The list of questions will give clues, as will the suggested methods for forming questions.

■ *Summarizer*—Taking into account the chapter and everything said in the group that day, the students in this role are to summarize the group's most important conclusions. Their task is to take all the bits and pieces of information that have been swirling around them and the group and mentally step back far enough to see the big picture. You can explain that their task is analogous to the following situation: when people look at a painting one inch from the canvas, they see it as a mix of colors, brush strokes and textures, but they cannot attribute any meaning to it. As they move back, they see the bigger picture and the meaning of all those swirls of paint. The same is true for history— students must step back to see the picture they have all painted.

*Dividing the Period.* The teachers will not be the only people responsible for presenting each day. Every group member will contribute each day according to his or her role. The teacher's contribution will probably take the most time, however. A few ways to divide the period for reports are shown here:

|  | *Case 1* | *Case 2* |
| --- | --- | --- |
| Teachers (2) | 25-30 minutes | 20 minutes |
| Philosopher | 5-6 minutes | 7-8 minutes |
| Time traveler | 5-6 minutes | 7-8 minutes |
| Questioner | 5-6 minutes | 7-8 minutes |
| Summarizer | 5-6 minutes | 7-8 minutes |

Each person must be prepared to contribute for at least this long for each role. On any given day, any given role might be the most important and take more time. Some roles may be more difficult for certain subjects, but every role is important every day.

Some of the roles tend to overlap in places. This overlapping is inevitable, but if students are to gain the most from each perspective, the unique aspects of each perspective must be developed to their fullest.

Although the roles other than the teacher involve shorter reports, these roles will take considerably more thought to prepare. They are the meat of the final presentation that each group will present to the other groups.

With these roles the topic will be covered from a number of viewpoints, all of which require different kinds of thinking and different skills. Different roles for different subjects can be substituted here. They do not have to be roles, either; they can be specific problems or questions that must be answered, all of which can be varied for different courses, classes, or units.

*Outlines.* Each person will present his or her role and make the final presentation by using an outline. No one will be allowed to read from the book or try to wing it. This outline is to be a true outline. Each line of the outline should contain not much more than a phrase, at most a sentence or two. The key words will organize and trigger the students' thought. An outline forces students to rely on their brains and trust them.

It is important that students not read reports, for reading negates the goal of thinking on one's feet in a social situation. At first the reporter could give another student in the group a more extensive outline of the teacher's presentation and then serve as prompter. This student could follow along and if the reporter gets hopelessly stuck, the prompter could say something like, "What about . . . ," mentioning the next substantive issue on the outline.

*Putting It All Together.* At the end of each day and for the entire fourth day, each group will organize all the information into a presentation. Each group will have the contributions of all group members, each of whom has approached the material from a number of different directions, with which to work. From all of this, each group will put together a presentation that each member can use. Each person can add or subtract material for his or her actual presentation as he or she sees fit.

Summarizing, organizing, outlining, and cooperating are all important here. Perhaps this portion of the activity will take more than one day. The number of days allotted will determine which skills will be emphasized. If you schedule one day, summarizing skills will be required; if you schedule two days, more orientation to detail will be required.

As part of the fourth day, each group wll choose the thirty best questions that its members asked and answered in their various roles. These will be the raw material for the second day of their presentations to the other groups.

The first phase, then, amounts to four days of researching and practicing for the big day (in phase 2), when each member of the group will teach an entire group for two days. Phase 1 is a type of boot camp, or training camp, in that it requires shorter presentations from all the students but allows them to try their hand at all aspects of the upcoming job—i.e., playing all the roles and sharing in each task leading to a final presentation.

A word of warning: avoid giving students too much to do or, equally important, giving them more to do than you can monitor and organizationally control. Construct your exercises so that you can shed skins if need be without affecting the integrity of the whole exercise. Sometimes you may have to sacrifice some parts for the sake of the whole. You have to remain flexible and constantly vigilant as to what is working, what is not, and whether or not the students are overburdened or underburdened.

You have to anticipate continually what can go wrong and how to prevent it. At the same time, you have to leave the format open enough that every thought and action is not artificially structured. The key is to have escape routes available and to have preventions broad based and nonprescriptive. The degree to which an activity can have a laissez-faire structure depends on the students and how much practice they have had.

### Phase 2: Intergroup Teaching

On a group's assigned date to teach, the members will each go to another group. As the representative of their group, each member will teach this new group the assigned chapter. The entire class will read that chapter, or particular assigned pages, the night before a chapter is to be presented.

How much of a chapter to have students read in just one or two nights is an issue. With most textbooks, the entire chapter is probably too much. You may want to have a plan of designated pages or topics that must be read. Or you can allow the group teachers to determine the amount, for after all, it is desirable to have the reading complement their presentations. Each approach will put a premium on different kinds of reading skills: summarizing, skimming, browsing, picking out the main themes, seeing the big picture, or discriminating details. Perhaps a few skill days can be dedicated to these reading strategies. Remember that a skill day can be inserted anywhere in any of these activities.

An additional point to emphasize here is that although the second phase devotes only two days to each chapter, those two days do not have to be the only exposure the students have to that material. If the curriculum plan calls for more coverage, you can go back and overlay another activity on top of those same topics; you can lecture or plan another activity. You could use the two days as an overview, as the structural framework on which more can be built. Also, you yourself can teach between each group's presentations to round out the missing details or perspectives. Last, you can also extend the length of the presentations.

Each student will teach for two days. On the first day the students will give their group's presentation. At the end of the period they will assign five questions to each student (from the list of 30-50). Each question should involve facts from the chapter and force the student to incorporate those facts into a far-reaching analysis of a concept.

Each person must formulate two possible answers (positive and negative) for each question. This exercise will involve research, and the students must be ready to answer those questions the next day. The group-teacher will call on students, the group will discuss each point of view, and the group-teacher will integrate it into the overall presentation.

On the second day, the entire period wll be spent in discussing these questions. The teacher should have planned these questions with a grand design in mind: they should build toward some main theme that ties them all together. The teacher must do this tying together constantly as the discussion moves along and especially at the end.

Again, questioning! This period will exercise a student's ability to lead a discussion, play devil's advocate, relate everything that is said to everything else that has been said, and keep everything channeled toward achieving comprehensive understanding of the chapter. These particular skills could be taught at some point but, again, every skill cannot be taught in every activity. If students encounter great difficulty, or even fail, at carrying out particular tasks, this failure is immensely valuable. It can lead them to do better next time—after the students have had a chance to experience it, discuss it, and perhaps be taught a lesson about it.

In any case, at every point in every activity you must have a plan for what you will do if a certain task is unworkable in the given circumstances. This plan, naturally, should be an alternative method of achieving the same lessons.

*Summary of Responsibilities During the Activity*

The first resposibility is preparing and making presentations. This involves preparing for the next day's role, reading the entire chapter and pondering how it all ties together for the individual presentations, writing down all information, questions, and answers that the students will contribute to the group the next day, studying and practicing the group's presentation, and making the presentation.

The second responsibility is listening and contributing to the presentations. This involves reading the chapter being presented to the group, answering the questions that the teacher has assigned, and contributing these answers and thoughts as the teacher asks for them the next day.

At the end of the activity the students will be responsible for a final product that will involve their impressions about their learning in many areas of the activity. Most of these activities require an introspective summary by the students, which forces them to analyze their own thought processes in relation to the activity's goals. The following questions will help them in this regard: What did you learn about history as a concept? What did you learn about groups of people? How do they work? How do people behave? What did you learn about learning? What did you learn about yourself?

*Grades.* All grades are to be given on the basis of cooperative behavior and performance among group members, teachers, and groups. Each student's grade depends in large part on everyone else's performance. Thus, it pays for students to cooperate, help, and motivate one another. On the other hand, if someone does not pull his or her load, he or she will be hurting everyone else, not only in the group but in the entire class. This is how the grading works.

In the first phase each person in the chapter group gets the same grade—a group grade. This grade is determined by: (1) the performance, effort, and cooperation of all members in the preparation stage of the presentation—i.e., first four days and (2) the average of all individual presentations of each group to the other groups.

Starting with the second phase, the students listening to each presentation being given to their group are graded on the average performance of the students in *all* groups. Each student will thus get the same grade for each presentation. All students will determine what that grade is.

So, at every step of the way, if anyone goofs off, he or she will hurt everyone's grade. If each student does his or her part in each group, the teacher will look good, and if each teacher does his or her part, the group will look good. And when all the groups look good everyone looks good—"A"!

[1]Bloom, P., Ed. (1977). *Taxonomy of Educational Objectives,* Handbook 1. New York: Longman.

# 6

## Exercise 2: Nonegocentric, Historical Thinking

The organization of this activity is not much different from that of the others. Like all of them, it shows that many purposes can be accomplished through the same basic procedural foundation. In this case (a history class), the intent is to have students look at history nonegocentrically and emotionally, so that they develop a bond to what they are studying. This goal is an obvious overlay on the built-in mechanisms ensuring social interaction and mastery of the subject matter. This overlay is constructed by using the activity's introduction to provide a particular orientation for the students and by adjusting the journal contents to reflect that orientation. At the same time the activity can function independently of any such overlay. Nonegocentric thinking is not the only lesson of this activity; it is only an orientation that, as a procedural overlay, can be altered and adapted to any purpose.

The content for this activity as presented here was derived from a course entitled "Western Man."

## Introduction for Students: Twentieth-Century European History

In terms of the time scale of history, the twentieth century is more immediate, seemingly more relevant, and certainly more familiar. Students can more readily identify with the events, characters, and ideas they are studying. Some of the heroes of this period of history are still among them; their parents and grandparents are living testimony of this history; and the world they live in is a recognizable offspring of this history.

Of course, relevant history does not start only when students can recognize it, but the closer history is to them in time, the more emotional investment they have in it. This emotion is important because it usually accompanies questions about history and is often the driving force behind their attaining answers. We will make use of this more personal and emotional character of the immediate past in this exercise.

## Goals and Skills

The goals of this activity are as follows:

- to speak in public,
- to gain mastery of the events and ideas of a certain period,
- to learn research and organizational skills,
- to get response from classmates and to learn from one another,
- to learn to ask relevant questions that lead to meaningful inquiry, discussions, and conclusions,
- to learn to follow a theme through time,
- to learn how to fit historical themes together to gain an overview of the mood of an era,
- to connect yesterday to today and vice versa,
- to learn to discern philosophical issues in events and see their larger ramifications for history and humankind as a whole,
- to relate to history as the record of lives of people, not just random events,
- to locate forks in the historical road and to notice other paths we could have taken,
- to escape our self-centered mind-sets to become aware that the rest of the world today and in ages past does not share our values, goals, concerns, and lifestyles,
- to spark some emotional as well as intellectual awareness of the lives and times of other peoples,
- to add another dimension of perception—historical—to our present lives, and
- to improve our skills.

The skills emphasized here are shown with the specific activity planned for practice of these skills:

| *Skill* | *Activity* |
|---|---|
| Reading | Text reading |
| Writing | Keeping a journal |
| Speaking | Teaching the class and leading discussions |
| Discussion | Preparing discussion questions and discussing them |
| Group cooperation | Depending on everyone to work for a good grade |
| Organization and research | Preparing teaching presentations |
| Self-awareness | Keeping a journal |
| Leadership | Serving as group leaders |
| Thinking with different parts of ourselves | All phases of the activity |

The goals here are dual: (1) to see history—and, consequently, the present—through a nonegocentric lens and (2) to imbue thinking with an emotional-intuitive component. These goals are simultaneously contradictory and complementary—contradictory in that the nonegocentric view seeks to divest oneself of self in order to understand other times, complementary in that one must go deep within oneself to find the core shared with all humans of all time, to connect emotionally to people, and to ground an intellectual curiosity in an emotional investment.

This dual direction will shape your presentations and emphases in instructing students in this exercise. Make sure they know they are supposed to think with other parts of their being. Admittedly, this is a fuzzy concept but no less real.

## Organization

The class will be divided into groups of six persons. The number in each group and the number of groups depend on how many students are in the class. This activity, like the others, does not require a certain number of people in a group to make it work.

Each person in each group will be assigned a chapter from the text to teach to the rest of the group (a calendar is included with this handout). The group is a miniclass, and each student will take turns being the teacher.

The teaching assignment need not be an entire chapter; it can be any length of text. A chapter is a convenient unit but not necessarily the best amount in all circumstances. It may be too much for some students, but it may bring out the best in other students.

Shorter assignments—a section of a chapter or 5-10 pages—would be easier for many students to digest and would be an easier transition exercise if this was to be one of their first attempts at these activities. Also, with shorter assignments each teacher could more easily know what previous teachers had taught in order to give their own presentation, which would be a continuation of the other presentations.

A number of class periods (1-5) will be devoted to preparation and research. The number of periods devoted to research depends on several considerations. First, if you are going to use this opportunity to teach research, teaching, and organizational skills, then the number needed will be greater. Second, the shorter the teaching section of the chapter, the fewer periods needed to prepare. Last, the flow and organization of the class affect the number. If this exercise is integrated into a series of similar activities, it will require less preparation; if not, it will require more.

Each teacher will teach his or her class for two days. The activities to be included in each of those days are noted here and will be explained later.

■ The teacher will assign one-third of the chapter's pages each night for reading (one-third the night before the first day of teaching).
■ Each teacher will give a ten-question, fill-in-the-blank quiz on that reading each day.
■ The teacher will teach the group that day's lesson.
■ The teacher will have prepared discussion questions to ask the group during or after the presentation. The goal is to lead a discussion, not merely present a lecture.

- Each member of the group will also have prepared five questions for discussion based on the reading or his or her own research.
- The journals will be read and discussed.
- If these activities run short, the rest of the period will be filled with one of the following activities: (1) starting the next night's reading; (2) writing in the journal; or (3) writing, reading, or researching for each student's class presentation.

The number of days devoted to the teaching assignment depends on the length of the chapter and the depth of expected coverage for which each student is responsible. The assignment can be made shorter or longer, but in whichever direction it is altered, other parts of the activity must be altered proportionately.

All the activities are designed so that everybody will be required to participate every day and to be responsible for both the factual and "human" content of the reading. This goal is achieved by a multidimensional combination of skills such as reading, writing, questioning, speaking, memorizing, and analytical, hypothetical, and summary thinking. As you can see, enough elements are distributed among enough people so that any group should be able to work for an entire period. In fact, you may even have to peel away some portion of the requirements so that they can be accomplished in one period.

Each day each group member will take a quiz on the previous night's reading. Members will exchange these papers, correct them, and hand them in to the group teacher. The grade for this assignment is ten points per day.

Until the students get some practice at making up quizzes, instruct the teachers to make them easy or limit the kinds of questions they can ask. Students often consider a good question a trick question, or sometimes they ask questions that are too specific and not at all important. The purpose of the quiz is to teach students to recognize the most important facts in the reading and to understand why that information is important.

The way the teachers shape the questions indicates whether they understand why that fact is important or how it fits into the theme of the reading.

Taking time to teach how to make good quiz questions is not a waste of time for anyone but a lesson in recognizing primary themes and ideas. Remember that every part of every activity is meant to teach thinking skills. You must approach it as such, let the students know what the skills are, and explain and modify these elements as you proceed so that they do indeed serve this purpose.

Each day each group member will write in his or her journal. These entries can be approximately one page (or as many pages as he or she likes). The journals will be handed to the group teacher each day. That teacher will assign the following grades: no points if the work is not done, 7-10 points for the content and effort of work done. The teacher can use these journals for discussions or simply grade them. They do not have to be graded until the day after the teacher finishes his or her teaching assignment.

### Grades

The purpose of the journals (explained in detail below) is to stimulate nonegocentric, historical thinking. They cannot be judged objectively. Thus, it is the students' efforts that are important. For that reason, teachers will not be allowed to give fewer than seven out of ten points as a grade unless a student does not do the assignment at all, in which case the teacher will give a grade of zero.

The advantage of this system is that no one is penalized for an arbitrary or uninformed grading by any particular teacher on a particular day. But the points add up, day after day, and the cumulative results should not be seen as insignificant by the students. At the same time, no one should feel victimized, because different teachers are grading every day as the group duties rotate, thus producing a very "democratic" grade. A student's ideas are judged on average by a number of people, thus negating, over the long run, the chance that bad grades may result from differing ideas or world views between a student and a singular, grade-giving figurehead.

Grade inflation is also a possibility, of course, but the lower limit on grades helps students to view one another's work critically without fear of reprisal. Having only a three-point range makes differentiation of quality fairly easy to determine. Learning to differentiate quality is a valuable discriminatory skill for students, and this exercise couples the opportunity to do so with a meaningful and practical responsibility so that the opportunity is taken seriously. The constant and immediate response in both discussion and grades then reinforces the development of these skills.

*Grades for Group Members.* Each day, each member of the group will turn in five discussion questions. They must be discussion questions that evoke opinions and argument, not one-word answers. If students have prepared all five, they get five points per day. Four questions are worth four points, three questions worth three, two questions worth two, and one worth one.

These questions must be handed in whether or not they are actually used in a discussion. Their purpose is not only to help students understand the reading but also to be used as an emergency resource in case the group teacher runs out of things to teach for the day. If the group members make it easy for the group teacher and are ready to bail him or her out, he or she will be more likely to help them when it is their turn to be the group teacher.

In this exercise the discussion questions are designed primarily as a fail-safe device for the group teacher, but this fact does not lessen their importance as learning tools for the student. The group teacher will probably have to fall back on them quite often, and you might want to require that they be used.

The grading scale depends only on whether the questions have been prepared, not on their quality, for three reasons.

First, the group teacher already has enough to do without having to make time-consuming quality judgments on each question. Second, a basic "bootstrap" principle is at work here. By taking the initiative and doing what is required, the students will be rewarded for effort, without fear of ego-threatening evaluations. In other words, they have the opportunity to pull themselves up by their own bootstraps. Last, as the instructions state, these questions are a resource to help the teachers with their presentations. This aspect is an appeal to the students' altruism. Granted, there is also an element of self-interest here because students will help the teacher if their help will induce the teacher to help them when it is their turn to teach. Thus, cooperation derived from a balance of self-interest and altruism is achieved—not a trivial thing to ignore when you are designing activities.

One last organizational observation comes to mind here. If a group teacher seems to have too many grading responsibilities in this exercise, you could schedule a different person to grade different products each day: one person could grade the journal, one the quiz, and one the discussion questions.

Each grade will be marked on the teacher's grade sheet. This sheet will be turned in to you at the end of each group teacher's assignment. Also to be turned in to you by the group teacher will be the graded journals and all students' discussion and quiz questions, which will later be used for make-up work and could also be the basis of a unit test.

*Grades for the Teacher.* The grade for the group teacher comes from the class teacher and from the group members. You will sit in on, tune in, and observe all teachers. You will be looking for answers to specific questions:

■ Are the group teachers covering most of the important points of each chapter?

■ Are they bringing in information from other sources to supplement the text?

■ Have they done enough preparation, and are they organized?

■ Are they involving the entire group in discussions and other planned activities?

- Are they keeping the group members on task?
- Are they making an effort adequate to the assignment?
- Are they organizing their presentation based on the goals of the assignment?

This exercise is worth 200 points.

The group members' grade for the group teacher is based on their critique of the teacher's performance. The last fifteen minutes of the teacher's last day will be spent writing this critique and assessing a grade of 70-100 points for the entire three-day period. These critiques are to be handed in to the class teacher. Their average will be the students' grade for the group teacher. The critiques will be returned to the group teacher after the grades have been recorded. This exercise is worth 100 points.

At the end of the unit there will be an essay test, which will be worth 150 points.

Extra credit worth up to thirty points will be given for certain activities; this will be explained later.

In this exercise a lot of grade points are coming from a lot of directions. To organize them in the students' minds, it is a good idea to give each student something like the following copy of what might appear in your grade book. In this way, the

Figure 6.1. *Sample of Teacher's Grade Sheet*

| Teaching From: | | Journals | | | | Quiz | | | | Questions | | | | Essay | Extra Credit |
|---|---|---|---|---|---|---|---|---|---|---|---|---|---|---|---|
| Group (100) | Mr. L. (200) | (10) | | | | (10) | | | | (5) | | | | (150) | (30) |
| | | Day: 1 | 2 | 3 | ....| 1 | 2 | 3 | .... | 1 | 2 | 3 | ... | | |
| | | | | | | | | | | | | | | | |
| | | | | | | | | | | | | | | | |

students can keep track of their daily progress and can easily visualize their responsibilities.

You will have to cull most of these grades from the group teacher's grade sheet when they are handed in to you. The final essay will be graded solely by you.

As for grading the teachers, you will have to move around the class, sit outside the groups, and observe. You can simultaneously zoom in to one group while being aware of significant happenings in others. You should have a piece of paper with each teacher's name on it to record your comments, suggestions, criticisms, and evaluation. This evaluation, or an adaptation of it, should be given to each group teacher to review. It should be quite extensive because during a two-day teaching presentation you will be able to observe each teacher individualy for about twenty minutes, and all five or six teachers peripherally for the entire time.

# The Journal: "History in My Life"

A typical nonhistorical and egocentric view of many students is that they are born into a world that is already formed. They are socialized into a society without being consulted. Their ideas, norms, institutions, government, and technology are already established. As they interact in this environment, they tend to think of it only in its present form. They come to accept it and even take it for granted. They usually do not even consider that once it did not exist, that people had to dream up the ideas to make it possible, and that these ideas, no matter how commonplace they may be to us now, were once revolutionary. They do not easily see that our way of life today represents the choices between ideas made by people who lived long before us. Nor do students easily recognize that our social life and thought are not the way things must be or necessarily the best that they could be but simply the way we have made them.

To help students grasp these realizations and to achieve the goal of making history, and all learning, more personal, the students will be required to keep a daily journal. They are to ponder the history of their day-to-day life—the places they go, the way they are required to act, the things they think about, the way they think about them, the things that they are concerned about, the things they see people around them concerned about, the issues that appear important to society as a whole, the values of our and other nations, the conflicts in the world, and so forth.

As the students go about their daily activities, they might focus on specific topics like the following and ask similar questions:

- *Schools*—When were schools invented? Why? How were they organized? How did most people learn before schools existed?
- *Machines*—When did the world become so mechanized? What was life like before? How has history changed since then? How have machines contributed to progress? What moral issues do they raise?
- *Political values*—When did the idea of running for office get started? What other ways are there to get things done? What are the various political ideologies in the world?

These sorts of inquiries are endless. Students simply must ask some questions, answer some if they can, or offer an opinion. This material will then be used for discussion in the groups as it becomes relevant to topics they are discussing.

Journal entries should have three parts. First, they should describe the article, event, or thought that triggered the journal thoughts. Second, they will include a page on the student's opinions, questions, or answers to his or her wonderings. Third, students should try to relate their thoughts to the period their teacher is teaching. They may not be able to find absolute causes or answers, but they will most assuredly find many opinions on their observations, especially as the groups cover more and more history.

If a particular group of students does not have the ability or experience to complete this journal along with their other responsibilities, then the journal can be eliminated. The underlying principle is that exercises should be designed to challenge students but that if the challenge is too great, parts of the activity can be eliminated without damaging the activity itself.

Even if the journal itself is eliminated, the spirit of its purpose need not be. The students can still look at their reading from the perspective of relating their life today to that of the past.

## Attendance

These activities cannot be improvised. Attendance by every student is necessary to make the group work every day, not just when the student is the teacher. Six persons to a group is a good number for lots of personal interaction. Too many more than that and individuals get lost; too many fewer and the group loses its vitality, variety, and identity.

The attendance policy in each group is this: every student must be present every day. Work will be accepted only in the case of excused absences.

The written material—quizzes, journals, discussion questions, and essay—can all be easily made up, although the group teachers will have to turn in their quizzes so that you can give them as make-up work. The teaching, however is more difficult. If a group teacher is absent, the easiest thing to do is divide that group among the others, whereupon extra grade sheets should be given to the group teacher to grade these new students. These grade sheets would be given to the absent teacher when he or she returns.

Organizing a make-up for a scheduled teaching presentation does present problems. Substitute activities (papers, outlines, and so forth) are possible, but these do not accomplish the same social or speaking goals that are the main reason for the activities in the first place. Also, you do not want substitute activities to be seen as preferable or as an easy way out, thus encouraging fabricated "excused" absences.

One possibility is to schedule a make-up day (if needed) into the middle and at the end of an activity. Since the teacher's group has already heard a presentation for that chapter when they visited other groups, the teacher's responsibility on a make-up day should be changed to leading a review session of all the chapters studied to date. In doing so, he or she can call on the expertise of all the other teachers, who are experts on their own chapters. If there are ony a few absentees, then a few groups will have to be combined. In the worst case, one absentee may have to lead a review for the entire class (but only for fifteen or twenty minutes because you do not want to penalize someone for having an excused absence). Also, the absent teacher could be given all the discussion and quiz questions of all the groups for all the chapters, which could be the basis of the review. But the teacher must try to lead and contribute to the discussion, not just read questions.

## Extra Credit

If students attend every day, hand in all work on time, contribute to the class discussions every day, and do not disrupt the group or the class as a whole, they will receive thirty points of extra credit for the entire activity. Both the group teachers (see grade sheet) and the class teacher will make these determinations.

Group leaders may receive extra credit of three points a day in addition to the thirty everyone else gets. Group leaders are chosen for several reasons:

- They deserve the honor by virtue of their grades;
- They asked for and need the responsibility. Therefore, by doing well and cooperating, the other students can help these people's grades and will receive extra credit for helping;
- Their behavior and attendance and effort has been consistent and improving.

The responsibilities of group leaders are varied. Basically they are overseers who make sure the activity follows the letter of the plan. They do not have to do anything unless something goes wrong and the teacher for the day does not correct it. They are there to promote cooperation among members, not to discipline anybody. Their role is to facilitate and mediate the activities. Another responsibility involves helping people with their presentations if they ask for it, giving general hints on organization, procedure, and support.

Students are always asking for extra credit, even those who do not need it. If you choose to provide a means for gaining extra credit, the above method does so in a more meaningful way than the usual research project. It is a method that: (1) requires everyday performance (not just one weekend) with practical classroom consequences, (2) helps everyone, (3) rewards effort and intent, (4) develops a skill (leadership), and (4) gives students a chance to help themselves, but in a format that is quite different from the type that got them in academic trouble to begin with (tests, papers, and so forth).

The reason for offering extra credit for this activity is that there are always some students with whom the teacher needs to establish good faith: "I'll help you if you will help yourself." Some students need for you to go out of your way first before they will understand the basic tenet of responsibility: "You simply have to do what is required, and you will receive your just desserts." Or, "You made your bed, now lie in it." These admonitions are supposed to teach that we are all responsible for our own actions, but to many students, put in this form, it is a negative lesson.

If students want to achieve extra credit, we should assume at first that they obviously realize the folly of their ways and recognizes that they must change. We should reward the realization while it is sincere, not punish it by saying, "Too late." It may be "too late" after you give a second chance, but it should not be the first time. Thus a positive lesson should be offered that rewards the intent and change of heart and allows the person to prove himself or herself now. Next semester may indeed be too late because bad semester grades could forever dampen the student's performance and his or her desire to try to change.

## Tips for Student-Teachers

The following suggestions, which derive from students' common mistakes, are to aid students in their presentations. This section can be presented to the students as a skill lesson in making presentations.

1. Know the material thoroughly, but do not try to memorize a speech. You have to present facts as a starting point, but do not get bogged down in the book's explanations and format. Explain each section that you are teaching in the way you understand it; try to think of it as if you are telling a story. Remember that you are not alone. Everyone else has read the chapter also, so if you are wrong or have left something out, someone else will explain it. As the teacher you are the center around which the learning will revolve, but you are not the sole source of that learning.

2. If you do not understand something, do not fake it—ask someone else in your group to clarify the issue. Then you can regain the direction of the group.

3. If you are lecturing, speak slowly, repeat yourself, and rephrase and reemphasize important points. The tendency is to start speaking at the speed of light and then go even faster after that. This tendency is usually a combination of two things: (1) being nervous and (2) reading from a text or notes. Do not read to the members of your group. Talk to them and with them. Try to explain ideas without your notes. When you are stumped and at a loss for words, everyone else gets a chance to think about what you have said, assimilate it, and maybe offer some opinions. You do not have to have a certain amount of material; you do not have to look or sound like an expert; you simply have to try to make people understand the major ideas and events.

4. Two days is a long time. Do not try to be the star the entire time. Try to think of imaginative ways to get the information across. Just because you are the teacher does not mean you have to imitate all the teachers you have ever had. Present the material in any way that you think is interesting, fun, educational, and not disruptive to the other groups.

5. Try to relate the events of the period to today.

6. Utilize the group's journals and discussion questions.

7. Use your text for maps, charts, or photographs.

8. Use outside resources—for example, school and public libraries.

9. Try to get every person to contribute every day.

10. Make sure you give the assignment.

11. Break up your presentations with questions, photos, maps, and so forth.

12. With all major events and ideas, discuss their relevance to human nature, world society, the world's problems, and the world's good points.

13. People have a peculiar tendency to look at history and recall only its tragic events. Try to emphasize what has gone right in history, what is right with people, and what is right with society. Contrast the reasons and events of despair with the reasons and events of hope.

14. Approach your period of history not only with a view to the specific events but also philosophically. What do these events say about the nature of man, the abilities of the brain, progress, survival, love, and so forth?

15. Approach the facts with empathy and emotion. Do not be merely a reader of sterile events. You are a human observer of and participant in human events. Put yourself in the place of the people you are studying. How would you feel and think in their situation? What were the people of the day thinking and feeling? What were their tragedies? What were their triumphs? Could you have endured their lives? Are you envious of their lives? What would they think if they could see how we turned out? Would they be happy or disappointed? Looking back, would they have thought all the killing was worthwhile? Did the cause they fought and died for ever come to be, or did they die in vain? Is war ever justified, or is it always in vain? Is the cause of the many superior to the life of the one?

16. The twentieth century is the first period in which photojournalism comes to the fore. Photographs are often the best way to get people emotionally involved. Another good way is with poetry or excerpts of prose that might relate to your topic. Do not forget music or art.

80202

17. Remember that in small groups you can do many things that would not be possible in a larger class. Utilize the small, intimate nature of your group to your advantage.

18. Back up and summarize new concepts so that you can put them in context.

19. Do not keep forging on without periodic summaries.

20. Avoid the pitfall of organizing the period so that you are all alone. Self-consciousness increases as the period goes along. You will feel that you are more and more alone and that no one is listening to you.

21. Keep integrating new information with information you have already given.

22. When you ask questions, pursue them until they are answered and a conclusion is summarized from the answers.

23. If boredom sets in, remember that a group lets boredom happen to itself. It is just as responsible—if not more so—than the teacher. This phenomenon is an example of the receptive mentality of most people. People are not used to being participants—they want to be entertained.

24. If you sense confusion or questions, encourage group members to speak up. If they do not, everybody will be lost.

LINCOLN CHRISTIAN COLLEGE AND SEMINARY

Sample Calendar of Presentation Schedule

| Group | Chapter | Date |
|---|---|---|
| **1** | | |
| Noah | 24 | Dec. 10, 11 |
| Erich | 25 | 12, 13 |
| Kellie | 27 | 14, 17 |
| Chris | 28 | 18, 19 |
| Jamie | 29 | 20, 21 |
| Debbie | 30 | Jan. 7, 8 |
| | | |
| **2** | | |
| Jay | 24 | Dec. 10, 11 |
| Kellie | 25 | 12, 13 |
| Cheryl | 27 | 14, 17 |
| Jennifer | 28 | 18, 19 |
| Steve | 29 | 20, 21 |
| Carnyta | 30 | Jan. 7, 8 |

Figure 6.2. Sample Grade Sheet for Student-Teacher

Teacher _____

| Student | Quiz (10pts.) | | | | Journals (10pts.) | | | | Questions (5pts.) | | | | Contributions (yes or no) | | | Attendance (X) | | | Disruptions (x) | | | TOTAL |
|---|---|---|---|---|---|---|---|---|---|---|---|---|---|---|---|---|---|---|---|---|---|---|
| | 1 | 2 | 3 | T | 1 | 2 | 3 | T | 1 | 2 | 3 | T | 1 | 2 | 3 | 1 | 2 | 3 | 1 | 2 | 3 | |
| 1. | | | | | | | | | | | | | | | | | | | | | | |
| 2. | | | | | | | | | | | | | | | | | | | | | | |
| 3. | | | | | | | | | | | | | | | | | | | | | | |
| 4. | | | | | | | | | | | | | | | | | | | | | | |
| 5. | | | | | | | | | | | | | | | | | | | | | | |

# 7

## Exercise 3:
## Analytical
## and Synthetical
## Thinking

This exercise is less regimented, allows more free choice, and involves more "free-lancing" by the students than some of the others. As a result, an activity such as this might be postponed until students have had more practice with this method of learning.

The exercise is structured into four phases, all of which are dedicated to finding a solution to a problem. The particular emphasis of this activity is exploring the idea of a world society, although any other idea can be substituted. The first phase, the most structured phase, requires students to choose a book to read and report on to their group every day. In the second phase, the students will recombine in groups by specialty based on the subject of the books, and each group will organize its own agenda to analyze the assigned problem. In the third phase the students will recombine again so that each group will be composed of specialists, each concentrating on a different subproblem. Here again, the groups must organize themselves in order to pursue the solution. In the last phase, each group will present its solutions to the class as a whole.

In the second and third phases the students must organize, analyze, and synthesize a vast amount of material. These periods have no schedule or format, and the students are on their own to figure out how to proceed. Since each of these phases involves a recombining of groups, students must do this twice—each time with different people, a different slant, and a different task.

The content of this activity as presented here is derived from a twelfth-grade sociology course.

## Introduction for Students: A World Society?

The purpose of this project is to take the first step in solving some problems. It is an exploratory project in that it attempts to define problems, become aware of them, and seek broad outlines for solutions. It is a committee project. Students will explore the idea of forming a world society, just as any decision-making body in government and business would explore a problem. They will determine the scope of the investigation and then assign specific committees to research and propose recommendations as to how to proceed. This division of labor maximizes the human resources for such a study and thus allows the most far-reaching analysis in a limited time with limited resources and a limited number of people.

You must make it clear that you are not proposing or espousing such a world society but trying intellectually to create something new out of present reality. In so doing you more acutely point to what the present societal structures are, how they work, what purpose they serve, what their strong and weak points are, and in what directions they might evolve. In addition, the act of creation is a powerful motivator; it elicits intellectual energy in much the same way as adrenalin. For most students, analyzing what exists is hardly as interesting as imagining what could be.

## Organization

Each student will get to choose the subject area and book that he or she wishes to learn about and read.

Allowing students to choose what they will study is always a motivator. Of course, this choice lies only within the boundaries of specific topics designated by the teacher. For students who are unfamiliar with the topics, the choice is to research something in which they think they *might* be interested. Sometimes they find they are interested, sometimes not. But these considerations aside, the more room there is for expressing one's interests, the more motivated the students will be.

The rationale for this choice is to correct a shortcoming of the last activity: no matter how humane the structure and process of an activity, it loses effectiveness if it does not concern something in which people have an interest or need or see a meaningful purpose. In other words, assigning a chapter of a text may not be the best way to guarantee a student's interest.

The goal is to investigate the advisability of beginning to plan for the creation of a world society. Up to this point in the course, students have seen how societies work in a limited geographical area; now, in relation to the world as a whole, they must see whether these conceptions are still workable or whether they need to be replaced by a new definition of *society*. If so, how many of the old ideas about society will they bring with them, and how many will they leave behind?

This exercise was developed as the culminating activity for a sociology class. The idea was to set up an environment that would make use of everything that had been learned about the structure and processes of society and force students to apply that learning in a hypothetical, policy-oriented situation. This format has many advantages:

■ It requires students to summarize and analyze all they have learned in a problem-solving context.

■ It requires students to extrapolate from what is (the present structures of society) to what is not (a hypothetical world society).

■ The problem is a complex one that will elicit many views. It is also a value-laden problem that will provoke self-analysis and lively discussion.

■ Regardless of students' individual opinions, the groups must come to a synthesis of ideas that could be the basis for a workable world society.

In the phases that follow, the number of periods has to be flexible. One group may finish a day ahead of another, or they all may be very slow. You will have to make adjustments as they proceed.

*Phase 1* (5-7 periods)

From the list of subjects and books at the back of this activity (others may be added), each student will choose a book that he or she would like to read. All books are to be interpreted in light of the future possibilities for societies and also to address the possibility of a world society. This is the goal toward which all individuals and groups will be working.

Students will be placed in groups of 4-6 with every attempt made to avoid duplication of books within a group. If duplication is unavoidable, some students should offer to change books.

Everyone will be reporting on his or her book every day. Each student simply has to read approximately twenty pages (or 45-60 minutes) a day and report his or her findings, feelings, and thoughts to the group the next day. This procedure continues each day until all the books are finished or everyone has read 150-200 pages of his or her book.

Everyone speaks briefly every day. This method not only minimizes the students' speaking responsibility each day but also maximizes the variety of information. No one presentation—good, bad, or boring—will dominate on a given day, as in the last exercise. This variety keeps the class exciting and targeted to students' ability and interests.

These progress reports will last from 7-10 minutes depending on how many people are in each group. Play it by ear. All members are aware of the group's responsibility—they should pursue it as they see best. Discussion of each report is welcome and encouraged. In fact, the more questions members ask or the reporter formulates, the more rounded, explicit, and comprehensive the final recommendations will be.

By the end of this proccess, each group will be exposed to 5-6 entire books. The class as a whole may have read 10-20 books, which represents a lot of information. In the third phase, the entire class will be exposed to all twenty books, not merely through isolated, sterile book reports but through a synthesis of the information in all twenty and of the questions, thoughts, and conclusions drawn from them.

To summarize, in this phase students choose a book to read from a comprehensive list. You want as many different books to be read as possible. Although you may have duplications of books between groups, you want to make sure there is no duplication within a group. Every day, each student will summarize, analyze, and speculate on his or her reading to that point and do so in the context of the goal of analyzing the possibility of a world society.

*Phase 2* (1-2 periods)

Next, the groups will reorganize by subject, as determined by the subjects of the books. (The first group was an interdisciplinary one with many books on many subjects but related to the overall topic of the activity.) A committee will be formed to examine each subject. For example the students in each group who were reporting on world ecological problems will now reorganize to become a separate group, and those students in each group dealing with security issues will become another group.

Students will have each been exposed to various viewpoints from the books on each subject, and now is the time to achieve some consensus and augment one another's findings. These committees will share their information, analyze it, and come up with possible solutions to the problem on a worldwide scale. Everyone should make a copy of this list of problems and solutions.

In this phase students who have done reading in the same subject will share and analyze information. If the books that were read were different and written from various viewpoints, this phase can produce a rounded, in-depth exploration of a subject or problem. Because in this phase all students are equals, as opposed to one student teaching others who do not know anything about the subject, there is the potential for much spirited discussion. The key to this phase is for each group to establish some kind of agenda for proceeding. The teacher can have a back-up organization, but the cooperative, organizational lessons will best be taught if the students plan their own agenda. Remember, if they have been doing this kind of group activity all semester, they should be able to see and solve these kinds of problems themselves.

*Phase 3* (2-4 periods)

Armed with this information, another new set of groups will be created by combining one specialist from each problem area, resulting in five interdisciplinary groups. Because each individual problem affects and is affected by all the others, these committees are necessary to achieve an integrated solution to global social problems. These committees will examine all the interconnections of the problems and their solutions and formulate a comprehensive plan for global world order.

As in the previous phase, the greatest difficulty will be for the groups to organize themselves, prepare an agenda, and divide responsibilities. After they accomplish this, their problem will be to synthesize a vast amount of material into a summary analysis and proposal.

Both sets of problems may require lessons, handouts, or practice somewhere within the activity or at some time prior to the activity, perhaps in a previous exercise. Often a handout of the steps in each process will be sufficient. These steps can be discussed at the beginning of each period or on designated lesson days.

The list of questions that follows puts forth various sorts of issues that the students may want to address. It is presented here to help orient the students' perspective in all three phases of the activity. These questions will help formulate exactly what the concept and problems of a world society are—or, for that matter, any society. Thus, make sure that these questions, or others like them, are read and discussed before the activity proceeds too far.

1. What are the global social problems?

2. What are their global characteristics?

3. What values do you see as important in a world society?

4. What kinds of institutions do you see as actors in this new society—nation-states, world institutions, private institutions, transnational organizations, international organizations, regional arrangements, superpowers, local communities, individuals?

5. How will global interests be emphasized without eliminating the separate values, goals, and beliefs of the various cultures, races, and ethnic groups?

6. How will diversity be preserved within unity?

7. What kind of rules will apply to arguing and solving conflicts?

8. How will progress toward achievement of your goals be measured?

9. What precise kinds of human behaviors will be part of this society?

10. What are the existing institutions, behavior, and values, and how will the transition be made from these to your vision of the world? Give a specific plan of action with respect to each.

11. How do you evaluate whether your plans are economically, politically, or culturally feasible?

12. What is the time frame of your plan?

13. Where do you begin—with the individual, community, nation, or world?

14. Who will make these decisions, measure the results, and uphold the rules?

15. How has the arrangement of the present world order contributed to the world's ills?

16. How can peoples' minds and values be changed?

17. How can people be persuaded to work toward one goal when they may have others? How can this be done without using force and thus creating as many problems as are solved?

18. How can national interest be transformed into global

interest and accepted without people fearing the loss of their identity and freedom?

19. What solutions to these problems can the present world order provide? Can it correct them as it is presently organized?

20. What are the dangers of global reform? How can the world be free of domination by one interest or one group of people and, thus, by one selfish view of the way things should be?

21. What values might people from other countries think more important than yours? Those of us with food, for example, may think peace is most important, whereas those without food may think food justifies waging war. Countries that have been colonial outposts may think national independence, sovereignty, and self-sufficiency are most important, while the oldest independent industrial nations may see their best hope in global interdependence because they need resources and markets all over the world.

22. What kind of social and political movements are necessary? Are they already underway?

23. Are there "termites" already eating away at the base of the present world structure?

24. Can the nation-state possibly be the organizing basis in a world where what one country does always affects another? Can one country willfully destroy ecology within its boundaries knowing that sooner or later the ecology outside its borders will be destroyed as a result?

25. Is the present idea of national security—protecting oneself by threatening and arming to blow up the world—functional?

26. Is the competition of the world-state system good or bad?

27. Define *social well-being*.

28. What rights of people must be protected and guaranteed?

29. How will education play a role?

30. What can each individual do?

31. How can the world move from using finite resources to renewable ones?

32. How can energy be distributed among countries?

33. How can accessibility to the world's scarce resources be redistributed? How can countries share without threatening their national security?

34. How can the gap between rich and poor countries of the world be closed?

35. How can the capital of the world be redistributed to allow all peoples the opportunity to support themselves?

36. How can management systems, technology, and education be made compatible with culture's beliefs, values, and structure?

37. How can technology be introduced where there is no education?

38. How can overpopulation be eliminated where large families are necessary to produce workers and take care of the elderly?

39. How can one country do anything without being imperialistic?

40. How can a country give aid without tying it to political or ideological aims?

41. How can people be given jobs where there is no industry?

42. How can enough food be grown without destroying the land with pesticides?

43. How can land be reclaimed where it has been destroyed?

44. How can the flow of people to the world's cities be stemmed?

45. How can the world be connected by communication?

These are just a very small number of the kinds of questions that the books the students read will bring to their attention.

*Phase 4* (2-5 periods)

Each interdisciplinary group will then make a presentation to the entire class, outlining its solutions. The presentation will cover the following major areas:
- the values and goals of the projected world society,
- the problems of this world society,
- the present structure for solving them,
- the transitional steps,
- methods of measuring progress toward goals,
- the structures, organization, institutions, authorities, and rules that will exemplify this global society.

This outline of what must be covered guarantees that the content of the activity is examined from many perspectives. As with the preceding list of questions, it provides a certain structure and points the students in a certain direction. Together the questions and presentation outline form a content framework and give students a grounding point from which they can view and interpret the wealth of information with which they are dealing.

# Grades

The grades for this exercise are to be cooperative—that is, everyone will get the same grade based on the effort and performance of every other person. This grading system is itself a lesson for students, and the following parallel should be drawn: if, as this project is exploring, there is to be any possibility of a world society, people of many nations and cultures will have to cooperate with one another to reach this common goal. Before nations can cooperate, people must cooperate. If only a few people selfishly pursue their own interests, everyone else may do so also out of self-defense. The same is true with nations: one country will not unilaterally cooperate to disarm if just one other country is going to maintain a nuclear stockpile.

If everyone, on average, does a good job, then everyone will get an "A." If everyone does not, then no one will.

# Suggested Topics and Books

The following lists of topics and books (of which there are many more possibilities) can be presented to the students to help them narrow their focus and choose an area of interest. Some topics for study include the following: the environmental crisis, hunger, energy, military preparation, the rich-poor gap, population growth, multinational corporations, global economy, supranational institutions, education, consciousness, poverty, and communications.

It is important to remember, in view of so many topics and books, that any issue can be substituted for the one given in this particular presentation of the activity.

*The Aquarian Conspiracy,* Marilyn Ferguson
*The Closing Circle,* Barry Commoner
*Creating Alternative Futures,* Hazel Henderson
*Diet for a Small Planet,* Frances Moore Lappe
*Energy Future,* Stobaugh andd Yergin
*Food First,* Frances Moore Lappe and Joseph Collins
*Future Shock,* Alvin Toffler
*The Limits of Growth,* The Club of Rome
*Operating Manual for Spaceship Earth,* R. Buckminster Fuller
*The Population Bomb,* Dr. Paul R. Ehrlich
*The Poverty of Power,* Barry Commoner
*Small Is Beautiful,* E. F. Schumacher
*The Turning Point,* Fritjof Capra
*World Without Borders,* Lester R. Brown

**8**

# Exercise 4:
# Evaluative
# Thinking

The emphasis of this exercise is on writing and evaluative thinking. The activity itself differs from the others in that it requires a presentation to the entire class, not just to small groups. Thus, it is both a good transitional exercise into group learning and a welcome change of pace offering all the rewards that accompany the techniques of students teaching one another.

The evaluative feature, however, distinguishes this activity from others. Although all involve students evaluating and grading one another, this one actually teaches the art of evaluation while at the same time providing numerous, in-depth opportunities for practice. These evaluations are to be extensive analyses and are to be written. The goal is not only to develop a discerning and analytical mind but also to enable students to offer sympathetic, constructive help to fellow students with respect to their writing and speaking.

Writing is also heavily emphasized here. The impossibility of providing students with enough writing practice has always been one of a teacher's biggest frustrations. It simply is not possible for one person to constructively evaluate many papers per week, so not much writing can be assigned. If it is assigned but not graded, then the assignments are not taken seriously. The format presented here requires an hour of writing every three days from everyone—an impossible requirement if there were not many teachers to evaluate the work.

The emphasis of the writing is, at first, simply to practice writing. The goal is to alleviate fear of writing and to experience the development and communication of ideas that it affords. Lessons on grammar, style, and sentence construction can be filtered in gradually, but that kind of emphasis is reserved until after these initial goals are realized. This approach may differ from many teachers' philosphy of how best to teach writing.

This activity has been used in both history and sociology courses, but its content is not specific to any one course.

## Organization

The class members will be divided into pairs. Each couple will be responsible for presenting a chapter from the text. Chapters will be assigned but may be traded by mutual agreement and notification to the teacher.

Each presentation shall consist of two days of presentation and one day of class writing. The writing assignment will be an essay question developed by the student-teachers and designed to elicit opinions concerning the topic they presented. These essays should be designed to include both the information of the chapter and the presentation and to develop opinions based on that information. The writing assignment will last for 35-40 minutes.

The remaining 10-15 minutes of the writing session will be spent with each student writing a critique (both positive and negative) of the teachers' presentation and their formulation of a thought-provoking essay question.

Each teacher will thus have a meaningful critique from every person in the class. One concern is that students will "rubber-stamp" grades for one another. In this case, however, they will be graded on their grades of one another, so their evaluations will be much more meaningful. The students will learn critical thinking, and the teachers will translate the results of that thinking into improvement in their group presentations.

The student-teachers will collect the papers and have four days to critique them. Each teacher will read each paper and write his or her own comments. At least one good point and one bad point should be noted in every paper. These comments are to be written on a separate piece of paper and attached to the essay. The teachers may make any notations they wish on the essay, but each should use a pen of different color.

The teachers will discuss with one another each paper and make a joint statement changing or affirming the individual comments. If there are no changes, this statement will be quite short. If the teachers influence one another's opinion, it may be quite long. (The teachers' task here is similar to that of the movie critics Gene Siskel and Roger Ebert on their television show.) Together they will decide on a grade.

From the papers as a whole, the teachers will pick a number of ideas they think are the best. They will copy these down exactly and put the question they relate to on the top of the page. The student's name will be put next to the quotation. These "best of the best" student ideas will be compiled and distributed as the class's own "text."

The rationale here is that so many good ideas being generated in classrooms are never acknowledged or shared. They remain buried forever in a pile of papers, seeing the light of day only once, briefly, as they pass beneath the teacher's red pen. Unless we teachers bring all the substantive ideas into a public forum, we are not creating situations that have maximum learning potential. We are implicitly saying that only ideas originating from the teacher are important and that they are important for only one reason—grades. The message is lost that ideas are valuable for their own sake and that worthwhile learning comes from everybody and everything if suitable conditions exist for the interchange of ideas.

Some people have more difficulty verbalizing their ideas than writing them. These people may get good or great grades, but they sit in silence in a traditional class situation, while the "talkers" steal the limelight and exert a disproportionate influence on the thinking in the classroom. Many students would benefit from these "quiet ideas."

Some students do not excel in either talking or writing. Their self-esteem is practically nonexistent. To bring their ideas to life in this way offers a publically reinforcing boost that is personally nonthreatening.

If you use this selection process in all your activities, you could accumulate and organize these ideas in a "textbook" at the end of each activity or just once or twice a semester. One problem to be aware of is that the ideas of some students may be left off this list. Then the opposite result would occur—those students would become more withdrawn. Making sure to acknowledge one idea from each student would solve this problem but might cheapen the value of the ideas chosen. The best approach is to keep track of students' good written ideas throughout the semester, bring them into discussions whenever possible, and attribute them to the students. In some cases you may have to interpret and elaborate on an idea, but you can present it as though everything that you are discussing is a product of that idea. Over the course of the semester you can use several ideas from each student.

You could even set aside entire days for lessons that are spin-offs of students' ideas taken from their papers. This elaboration on their ideas may inspire them to think, "Gee, did I say that?" and motivate them to delve even deeper next time. The entire thrust of this technique is to convince students that you think their ideas are worthy of discussion and to give them a sense of true contribution to the class. As a result, the students will experience a feeling of power to influence—not merely be subjected to—the thinking and proceedings of the class.

After they have been graded and critiqued, all papers will be handed in to the class teacher, who will then critique the critiques. The papers handed in will be a package containing from each person in the class an essay and an evaluation of the teacher and for each student in the class an evaluation of the essay by the student-teachers. As described later in the section on grades, you then evaluate the evaluations of each student for the student-teacher and the student-teachers' evaluations of the students. In short, the students evaluate one another's performances (presentations and essays), and you evaluate the evaluations.

You will return the papers to the students, who will then, in light of this critique by the student-teacher, examine his or her own writing and thought-formation skills. He or she will then compile throughout this exercise a list of improvements or changes that he or she intends to implement in order to develop these skills. A short analysis of what each skill is, how and when it is used, why it is important to each person, how he or she knows it needs improvement, and the steps for improvement should be included with each item. This step is necessary because comments and feedback are useless unless thought about and acted upon.

The list will be handed in every two weeks to the class teacher, who will make comments.

In light of student critiques of the presentations, each student-teacher will then make a list of ways his or her public speaking and thinking can be improved. A short analysis of what each skill is, how and when it is used, why it is important to each person, how he or she knows it needs improvement, and the steps for improvement should be included with each item. This list will also be handed in to the class teacher.

These self-critiquing features are vital if students are going to internalize the lessons to be garnered from all this response. In our hurried attempts to journey through all the course material, we often do not give the students time to become acquainted with the vehicle that gets them to their destination—their thinking processes.

Our infatuation with content has led us to ignore the container. Our nearsighted focus on the content of a thought has duped us into ignoring thought itself. Consequently as we try to stuff more and more into this static container, we become frustrated, because it soon becomes full. Our nearsightnedness leads us to continue trying to force content in instead of trying to expand the container and reorganize what it already holds.

Thus, the introspective features will help students become acquainted with the possibilities that lie within so that they may better understand the possibilities that lie without.

## Grades

The work to be graded by the class teacher includes the presentations (300 points), the student-teachers' comments on papers overall (100 points), each student's critique of the presentation (50 points), and the participation of each student each week during the course (50 points per week).

The work to be graded by the student-teacher is each student's essay answers (50 points).

This lesson on evaluation will carry over into every other activity where students grading one another is required. The problem with any activity in which students grade one another is to structure the activity so that the grade means something, that it is not gratuitous, that both giver and receiver learn from it, and that it reflects reality. Until students become good at grading and evaluating, the trick is for the class teacher to give more points than the students do so that the final result will not be a farce. This mix can be altered to fit any student's level of ability to critique other students.

The other side of the coin is that if students are going to take evaluations seriously, they also have to feel that their critical opinions do make a difference and that your grade will not simply neutralize these. The good faith and trust built up between students and teacher is important to maintain. The grades you assign should say, "I believe you can do this assignment, you are smarter and more capable than the traditional set-up indicates, and I believe learning is a shared experience."

## Skills

In addition to evaluation, the activity exercises many skills. The following list enumerates these and indicates which facet of the activity focuses on each.

| *Skill* | *Activity* |
|---|---|
| acquiring knowledge | readings and presentations |
| writing | essays and evaluations |
| speaking | presentations, class participation |
| analyzing and evaluating | essays, design of essay and test questions |
| critical thinking | grading and critiquing essays and presentations |
| discussing | class participation |
| cooperating | preparation with partner |
| organizing | preparation of presentation |
| research | presentations |
| reading | text chapters |
| developing opinions | essays |
| self-evaluating | list of writing, speaking, and thinking improvements |

# Tips for Presentations, Critiques, and Essay Questions

The following tips for giving presentations, formulating critiques, and developing essay questions serve as the framework for skills lessons in speaking and evaluating. These can be discussed with students before, during, or after the activity; they can be used to help them in their evaluations of one another; and they can be used in preparing their own presentations. All the tips that appear here were derived from observing the performances of the class during an activity. The list will grow as you observe and notice other good and bad points, difficulties, and successes.

### Tips for Presentations

This list can be given directly to the students and can be supplemented with similar tips in other activities.

1. Obviously, getting enough information out of the chapters is not going to be a problem, but explaining it is. If you can explain the material, you will understand it. Explain it to the group in the way that it makes sense to you, not the way the book does it.

2. Write key phrases on the board to help you slow down and to highlight points.

3. Paraphrase and rephrase the most important points.

4. Explain a point in your own words after you have given an explanation from your notes.

5. Ask a discussion question to find out if the students understand so far. Do not panic. Make them respond. Do not answer your own question without at least some effort on their part.

6. Do not assume the students know much. Most do not even know the terms, let alone having read the assigned chapters.

7. Using the board will help break your nervousness.

8. Get the class involved. When you feel stalled, nervous, or confused, take the burden off your shoulders and ask questions, backtrack, or summarize so that everyone will be with you.

9. Back up and summarize new concepts.

10. Do not keep forging on without periodic summaries.

11. Do not get too specific. Your interpretation of more general topics might make understanding them easier.

12. Avoid the pitfall of organizing the period so that you are all alone. Self-consciousness increases as the period goes along. You will feel that you are more and more alone and feel that no one is listening to you.

13. Keep integrating new information with information you have already given.

14. Try to relate concepts to everyday experience.

15. Do not just give facts. Give opinions and generalize. Comment on ideas and major themes.

16. When you ask questions, pursue them until they are answered and a conclusion is summarized from the answers.

17. The hardest thing to do in front of a group is to think. If a student asks a question, you may find it difficult to listen to the question and answer it. You may already be wondering what you are going to say next.

18. If boredom sets in, remember that a class lets boredom happen to itself. The class is just as responsible—if not more so— than the teacher. This phenomenon is an example of the recep-

tive mentality of most classes. People are not used to being participants—they want to be entertained.

19. If you sense confusion or questions, encourage class members to speak up. If they do not, everyone will be lost.

20. Not only do you need to summarize concepts, but you also need to introduce important concepts. Do not just reel them off.

21. If the first day is difficult, remember that you can use the second day to correct your mistakes.

22. Your demeanor may convey feelings that you expect the class members not to believe you or that you expect them to be bored or uninterested. Act as if you are confident, even if you are not.

23. Take command. You are the leader. Tell the students exactly what you want them to do and see that they do it.

24. If the students were not animated the first day, you may have to put a bee in their bonnet.

25. The biggest impediment to presentations is the image students have of what they involve. Instead, they should concentrate on presenting and mirroring their own thinking processes of figuring out the material. To present a so-called polished product is to offer something that the class does not have the time or ability to understand. You may understand it, but only after much time and thinking. Help the students do the same.

26. Give an introduction to your chapter.

27. Do not fall into the routine of giving your presentation the way everyone else is, and do not use everyone else's presentation as your standard of excellence.

28. Remember, people generally do not interrupt and ask questions of a reader, but they do of a conversationalist, so do not read your presentation.

29. Talk to the class members as if you are telling a story. Their minds pay attention to stories; they don't want to miss the end. They cannot keep track of information that they cannot identify, and a story-like context helps them keep everything in perspective.

30. The presenter and students all will have done the readings, so you have a common base of knowledge and should be able to put together the big picture of the presentation. Students must not come to class thinking they will be given all the information; they must read it first.

31. Class members, do not let the teachers read. Make them speak in their own words. If they cannot, have them read a sentence or two and then explain it in their own words.

32. Class members will become upset if you do not come prepared to teach and also to discuss. If you renege on your teaching assignment, you are responsible for diminishing other students' opportunity to learn. One person's bad attitude can shortchange everyone.

33. Class members who come to class interested in or curious about the material will find speaking up much easier. Discussion merely for the sake of discussion is difficult. They must think about the reading enough to relate it to their own interests.

34. When you know something, it is easy to talk fast and assume that everybody knows what you are talking about. But to the learner, everything must be relayed slowly so that the information gets absorbed.

35. Do not read. Reading creates a certain atmosphere that is annoying and distracting. Perhaps this is so because people talk as they think. Reading makes the product—the presentation—seem finished, as if the thinking is completed. The class cannot relate if you give them finished products unless you keep going back and summarizing. When reading a textbook, one has to keep rereading; listening is even more difficult.

36. Do not give book facts. As you read the text, the facts must strike you one way or another. What are your reactions? Incorporate these into your presentation. Incorporate your emotions, humor, awe, and curiosity.

37. Talking is also different from reading because it does not lull the listener to sleep. Reading usually does not contain the pauses, punctuation, or voice changes that talking to the class does.

*Tips for Critiques*

The following tips apply to both the presentations and the papers.

1. It is easy to critique a person's ideas by saying "good idea," "good presentation," or "I don't like it." Such comments elicit momentary elation or disappointment from the recipient, but they do not really help him or her. Think about why something is good, why you like it, why you dislike it. People tend to listen and accept in a passive way. We should listen actively, thereby allowing what is being said to trigger our own ideas, which can lead in many directions. Active listening is the basis of evaluation.

2. Indicate which parts of the presentation were boring, incoherent, good, understandable, or well done. Which parts did you enjoy the most? Which did you dislike? Do you feel you have a grasp on the chapter based on the way it was presented? How could the presentation have been improved? How much class involvement was there? Did the presentation make its point? Did you learn from the presentation? Did the teacher use the text information in ways to stimulate ideas or just repeat it to you? Did you agree or disagree with the teacher's opinions?

3. It is difficult to make comments that are helpful—i.e., those upon which people can act. Most people find it easy to compliment people, thus reinforcing their self-image, but true improvement usually means change. Suggesting change is hard, especially because we feel as if we are attacking people.

4. It is hard to say anything about excellent papers except "excellent." It is easier to make an argumentative comment about something with which you disagree. If you agree, then you should play the role of devil's advocate. You want to make the students with ideas like yours think other ideas also.

5. For idea interchange on the papers, the critiques should make some statement about whether the grader agrees or disagrees with the idea. If a person presented these ideas to you in a conversation, would you argue, or would you agree and add your own comments?

6. Indicate when you do not understand.

7. Suggest other avenues where thoughts might lead.

8. Your comments are to be about ideas, not about style, grammar, or spelling. Some people cannot write well, but they can think. Critique the thinking, not the appearance of the paper (that will take care of itself with practice, of which the students are getting plenty).

9. Don't be harsh, demeaning, patronizing, or cruel. Your role is to help and to stimulate an exchange of ideas.

10. Try to recognize unique, different, and original ideas and point them out.

11. Is something missing from the essay or presentation? Pinpoint what is needed to make you fully understand what is being said.

12. Mention those ideas that you, the "experts," learned from others' papers. Do not merely sit in judgment, but listen also.

13. Point out where the presentation leaves you feeling empty or unfulfilled.

14. A critique can start with feelings and then move to an explanation of why you feel that way.

15. Critiquing involves the ability to step back and look at things even as you are involved in them.

16. Do not dwell on technical details. Concentrate on your big impressions from moment to moment during the presentation. What were you feeling and thinking?

17. What are your reflections on the presentation? Is it fitting together into a whole picture? Why or why not?

18. Do not dwell on only one facet of the presentation. Try to comment on several.

### Tips Concerning Essay Questions

1. Many students' first impulse is to make up questions that require memorization of the entire book. Information is not stored that way, however, nor does such sentence completion mean much anyway.

2. Frame your questions so that the question and its introduction are intellectualy challenging even if the actual answer is only a one-word answer.

3. Even objective tests should get at what you the test giver feel are the most important aspects of your presentation—those ideas that students will take home with them from this class and incorporate in their view of the world. Information that does not contribute to or is insignificant or irrelevant to this kind of understanding is a waste of time.

4. Correcting the tests yourself allows you to see how good or bad your questions were.

5. State your question precisely.

6. A poor question may point to areas you do not understand yourself.

7. Questions are important because in most lectures and conversations questioning does not occur and the information passes unexamined.

8. The answers to questions are also an indication of how well you got your point across.

**9**

# Exercise 5:
# Introspective
# Thinking

All the activities presented in this book were born of a desire to correct a perceived fault or shortcoming in traditional American methods of teaching. The activities attempt to improve, refine, or correct shortcomings in themselves or in prior activities, and this process of refinement is continual. The rewarding and inspiring aspect of these group organization formats is that the boundaries of possibility for refinement and evolution seem so much wider than other classroom organizations.

This activity attempts to capitalize on that characteristic. Its ulterior motive, aside from teaching an academic content, is to involve the whole person in the learning process, a process that in many classroom formats seems personless. The format includes controversial subject matter with value-laden issues (the content under study is social problems), an introspective journal concerning the nature of learning, and a procedure for group and self-analysis. These three elements, when combined in a performance context, stimulate many intellectual and self-revelations that would otherwise lie dormant.

The content of the activity as presented here was based on material from an eleventh-grade course entitled "Social Problems."

## Goals

The goals of this activity include the following:

- to give students information while analyzing the learning and the process,

- to teach students about problems in education, learning, and creativity,
- to give students the opportunity to speak in public,
- to give students the opportunity to research something in which they are interested,
- to engage classmates in discussions that are of their own undertaking,
- to teach students to ask relevant questions that lead to meaningful inquiry, discussions, and conclusions. This skill will be necessary in both the research and class discussions,
- to allow students to take an active part in their learning as opposed to being passive receptacles,
- to have classmates react to a peer's ideas,
- to facilitate students learning from one another,
- to teach students different approaches and methods of exploring a problem,
- to encourage students to use this learning, talk about it, form opinions about it, and ask questions about it,
- to teach groups to be an endless fountain of ideas. This ability is learned with practice. Even if things start out shaky, by the end of a week or two students will find that there is not enough time in the period to talk about the day's topic.

The goals, in general, echo many of those of the other activities. The distinctive elements here, however, are contained in the first two goals. At every stage students will be analyzing what they have done and how they have done it, an analysis tantamount to an examination of the processes of learning, thinking, and interacting. The understanding that results should then lead to improvement in all these areas.

Because of the introspective and personal nature of the students' analysis, their observations and revelations are infused with a great deal of enthusiasm, wonder, and excitement.

# Organization

Each student will choose two social problems from the list or others in which he or she is interested. The class will be divided into four or five groups or miniclasses. The first four class sessions will be devoted to research and preparation.

After this preparation period, the groups will formally meet for presentations, and each day one student in each group will be the teacher for the day for that group (an assignment calendar will be given out). Two presentations (about a week apart) will be made by each person.

In researching their topics, students should make use of the library, books, magazines, newspapers, television, movies, and their brains. They should bring materials to class on which to work. The class teacher is available for help, suggestions, and information.

This research will probably take a half hour to one hour of preparation per night.

Class structure can vary. One example of possible time allotments follows: teaching and discussing (thirty minutes); analyzing the group's performance (ten minutes); filling in the day's learning chart (5-7 minutes); and filling in grades on the grade sheet (1-3 minutes).

At the end of two weeks, each student will prepare ten questions (multiple choice and true-false) on each of his or her presentations. The students will then take turns asking the questions of their group. This is the unit test. They will total the score for each member for all these questions and determine the percentage of correct answers. This percentage is the student's grade.

Students shoud be encouraged to help one another. They should know what the next day's topic is and be thinking about questions they would like to discuss or opinions they would like to offer.

# Suggestions for Teaching and Discussions

The following suggestions are to be given to the students and discussed.

- Talk informally. "Show and tell" what you have learned.
- Prepare a good list of discussion questions. Prepare more than you think you will need. The following are the best types of questions for discussion: (1) divergent questions (open-ended questions that have no answer but stimulate creative and imaginative thinking) and (2) evaluative questions (questions in which you pass judgment on some action).

  The role of discussion leader is to present the problems to be discussed, present ideas and suggestions related to the problem, keep the discussion on track, request clarification when needed, summarize the thinking of the group as needed, and try to get everyone involved.

- Use a springboard for your presentation—a story, article, picture, joke—something that will get everyone excited and thinking.
- Start with a question that group members should write on for about five minutes. Read the answers and discuss them.
- Have a brainstorming session. Present a problem and have everyone think of every possible solution or related idea. These ideas are "off the top of your head"—they can be as wild as you like. Jot these ideas down and then analyze the list. Are there any solutions, patterns, related ideas?
- Present a case study and then discuss possible solutions.
- You might want to give an assignment the night before your presentation. It could consist of a question to think about and be prepared to discuss. In this way you will be assured that your students will have done some preparation to help your class go smoothly.
- Be sure to organize your presentation as a problem to be solved.
- Play the "why?" game. If your group comes to a standstill, attack this problem as a child does: just ask, Why? Whatever

the answer, ask again, Why?

These suggestions are to get you started. You can add any that you would like. Experiment; be inventive and creative.

## Analysis of the Group's Performance

If the activity bogs down, and it will at times, instruct students to discuss the following issues and the questions concerning the nature of learning (presented later).

- Discuss together why you think the activity is slowing down.
- Analyze the kind of questions being asked. Are they properly worded to produce discussion? Do they involve judgment, evaluation, controversy, or imagination?
- Are all group members contributing enough? How might they have been better stimulated?
- Would another approach to the problem have been better? What other approaches might have been tried? Why are these better and what avenues of inquiry would they have opened? Follow them.
- Discuss the techniques that everyone else intends to use. Will they work?
- Have the teacher explain why he or she chose that particular teaching method. Why did he or she think it would work?

## Outline of the Day's Learning

At the end of each period (or at home) students will spend 5-10 minutes answering these questions: What did you learn today from your teacher? From the discussions? From your analysis of the way the group interacted and learned together? About yourself? About learning? Any other comments?

This is to be a substantive analysis and should probably be about one page in length. This length is not required, but if students' observations are not that long, you should instruct students to ask more questions about themselves and their ideas to see whether these help round out and clarify their thoughts. This exercise will be turned in to the class teacher every day.

The outline of the day's learning is the most valuable product of this exercise. It is an informative resource for any teacher interested in developing effective teaching methods and concerned with diagnostic-prescriptive indications of a student's abilities and how to improve them. The learning profile that emerges can be the basis for the development or use of activities that individualize both approach and content for each student and that simultaneously reach the most students.

At the same time, the awarenesses that the students achieve often become catalysts for self-correction or self-transcendence. Awareness of these thinking processes and skills is the first step in developing them. The skills cannot be improved unles students are aware of them, and usually they are not.

## Some Questions Concerning the Nature of Learning

The following questions are to be presented directly to the students as a guide for writing about the day's learning and engaging in discussions and self- and group analysis. An entire period may be scheduled in the middle of the activity for a full-class discussion of this learning and assessment of the class performance thus far. More questions and observations may then be added to this list from the learning outlines.

If you choose this strategy, you should be prepared to analyze your own ideas and the organization and rationale of the activity. Students may question whether it is well-conceived or accomplishing its goals. It may not be, and students' comments may help reorient it. At the same time, their criticisms may be self-defensive, reflecting their own inadequacies or insecurities. You must learn to interpret their responses and proceed accordingly. You must also have a firm grasp of the activity's rationale (discussed in the first part of this book) so that you are able to respond to all evaluations, positive and negative, in the context of the larger philosophical and pedagogical perspective. This grounding is important for your ability to interpret an activity's events and observations.

The following questions are designed to help make students aware of themselves, their thinking, and the interpersonal and ideational processes in which they are involved in their groups.

### The Nature of Learning and the Educational System

1. What is worth learning, worth knowing?
2. Do you like to learn?
3. Are you a "television" learner—i.e., a passive learner?
4. Do you apply school learning to yourself, or is it separate and devoid of all possible relevance?
5. Are there some things worth knowing for their own sake?
6. Is there something worth knowing in everything?
7. Is there something interesting in everything? Can you relate everything in some way to your way of thinking to make it interesting to you?
8. How do you feel about having to assume an active part in your learning?
9. How do you feel about being able to define how and what you will learn? How do you explain the lack of desire among many group members to do so?
10. Does the observation in the previous question mean that learning about anything holds no interest?
11. Who or what is responsible for this lack of interest or desire? The student? The structure of the class? The structure of the school? The structure of the society? The teachers?
12. What are the implications of your answers to the previous question for the prospects for change in the structure of the educational system?
13. What do you enjoy doing? You had to learn this skill, so your enjoyment seems to depend on learning. If so, why do so many people stop actively pursuing knowledge after they graduate from high school or college? Or do they?

14. Do you feel that you need more or less direction in learning?

15. Do you have to have a reason—i.e., grades, punishment, or reward—to learn?

16. Is there any such thing as learning for the fun of it?

17. Do you think the fact that some students will do as little work as possible is a commentary on the American educational system? Has the educational system "taught" that the activities of this type of loose structure can be skipped for other nonschool activities? What, then, is the worth of these alternative activities that you so passionately would pursue instead? Why do these alternative nonschool activities have such attraction? How do you judge the worth of different activities?

### Group Dynamics and Personal Feelings

1. Did you feel differently about the students in your group before and after the presentations? Did you learn from these new associations?

2. Did your group develop cohesiveness?

3. Did you feel that you were playing a role, or were you unselfconscious and natural?

4. How did you feel as an individual or as a group when you finished your work long before the class period was over? Guilty? Confused? Bored? Was it a waste of time? Did you even care? Did you feel anything? What did you do about those feelings? Did the group continue to interact, but about something else, after the teaching stopped? If your group finished early, did you feel that you were empty? Did you feel that you needed or wanted direction from the class teacher?

5. Why do you sometimes reach a dead end in your groups? At what point does the difficulty occur? Why? Do you lose interest? Is the next step—i.e., analyzing what is going wrong—too hard? Is this step too foreign to you? Is this step too threatening to you—i.e., is talking about your performances too personal? Do you simply lack practice? Does the group lose leadership and direction after the student-teacher finishes the presentation?

6. If your group stalled, what was the feeling you had as everything stopped? Explore the conflicts inside you at this point. Did you feel that you were supposed to be talking and yet were not? That you were failing? Did you experience confusion?

*Your Feelings as a Teacher and as a Student*

1. How did you feel when the group did not respond enthusiasticaly to an idea about which you were excited? Did it hurt your feelings? Were you hoping that the students would be excited also and that discussion would take place without your having to do much preparation? Did you say to yourself, "Those dummies"?

2. How did you feel when you, the student-teacher, gave a presentation that involved the whole group for the whole period and then someone else gave one that lasted for only ten minutes? Did the experience make you want to goof off next time? Did you feel good about yourself in comparison? Do you feel cheated when you do not learn much in class? Whose fault is it?

3. How did you feel being the center of attention for fifty minutes? Did you feel good? Did you like it? Did it enhance or diminish your self-image? Did you feel alone or did you feel support? What were your thoughts? What did you think the students were thinking? Were you concerned about what they were thinking about you?

4. Did you as the student-teacher have problems with any troublemakers, uninterested students, or unprepared students? How did that make you feel—frustrated, annoyed, insulted? Did it make you try harder? Did you even care?

5. How did you feel about your role as a student? Did you help? Were you extra baggage? Were you happy with the ideas you contributed? If not, what should you do to improve your feelings about yourself?

*Peer Learning: Quality of Learning from Classmates*

1. How do you feel about the quality of what you learn from your classmates as opposed to what you learn from "real" teachers?

2. Do you feel that learning from your classmates is valuable or a waste of time? Why?

3. Do you feel that only what you learn from so-called experts is reliable enough to be worthwhile?

4. Do you feel that your real teachers are experts?

5. Compare your present feelings about the topics presented with your feelings before the discussions?

### Grading

1. How did you feel about grading other students?
2. Did you grade objectively?
3. Did you give in to embarrassment or peer group pressure?
4. Were you afraid of hurting feelings?
5. Do you think grades are a good measure of achievement?
6. Do you think grades should be used in school?
7. Are grades fair?
8. Does society need grades?
9. How else could students' work be judged?

### Teaching and Learning Techniques

1. What teaching and discussion methods work best?
2. What are your criteria for measuring the success of these methods?
3. Which methods produce the most interest?
4. Which methods produce the most learning?
5. Does your interest level correlate to the amount you learn?

## List of Social Problems

This or a similar list of social problems may help students choose a topic that interests them.

| | | |
|---|---|---|
| abortion | cities | deviance |
| age discrimination | consumerism | divorce |
| aging | courts/prisons | drugs |
| alcoholism | crime | education |
| alienation | culture shock | energy crisis |
| bureaucracy | death/dying | environment |

| equal rights | technology | shoplifting |
| farm problems | mental illness | suicide |
| food | military preparation | technology |
| health care | pollution | transportation |
| human rights | population growth | unemployment |
| industrial growth | poverty | violence/terrorism |
| inflation | resources | welfare |
| law enforcement | sex roles | world disasters |

## Grades

This exercise can be graded in two ways: (1) adding your own grade for the teaching presentations and (2) letting the students' grades for one another stand by themselves. In the first instance, your grade can carry enough weight to balance any padding or discrimination in the students' grades. In light of the results of the second case, however, this safety net is not usually needed.

In this activity, with so much analysis and discussion of group interaction taking place, a self-policing mechanism naturally evolves. Students who do good jobs want to be rewarded accordingly, and they are frustrated and angry when another group member gives a much weaker performance and receives the same grade. On the other hand, students who are given a grade that approximates or is the same as an obviously superior performance feel somewhat guilty and undeserving. The social setting and discussion of group actions brings these emotions out into the open and magnifies them, thus tending to objectify the grades to a much greater extent. In fact, they will usually correlate with yours.

Figure 9.1 is an example of a grading chart for students' use in grading one another and the group as a whole.

**Figure 9.1.** *Grade Sheet*

| Teacher | Date | Teacher's grade for students | Student's grade for teacher | Group's grade for itself |
|---|---|---|---|---|
|  |  |  |  |  |
|  |  |  |  |  |
|  |  |  |  |  |
|  |  |  |  |  |
|  |  |  |  |  |
| A.J. | 2/22 |  |  |  |
| Clara | 2/19 |  |  |  |
| Beth | 2/18 |  |  |  |
| Jenny | 2/17 |  |  |  |
| Damon | 2/16 |  |  |  |
| A. J. | 2/15 |  |  |  |
| Clara | 2/12 |  |  |  |
| Beth | 2/11 |  |  |  |
| Jenny | 2/10 |  |  |  |
| Damon | 2/9 |  |  |  |

# 10

**Exercise 6:
Social Adaptation**

This exercise combines many features of previous ones and as such is a good example of how activities can be built by mixing and matching parts of one exercise with others. This exercise was created by borrowing the full-period essays every third day from the second exercise, the daily minipresentations from the fifth exercise, the intensive evaluative spirit from the second exercise, and an extension of the group-combination ideas of the first and fifth exercises. The latter is the unique structural contribution of this activity and from which the activity gets its title.

After each student-teacher's presentation, which lasts three days, the groups recombine according to a group rotation schedule. Thus, every fourth period each student is in a group with all new people and a new teacher. This rotation keeps groups fresh, prevents the routine of habitual behavior as well as a pecking order from forming, and constantly challenges students to be themselves and to excel in the midst of new faces. (If you can do only a few of these activities in a semester, however, everyone will certainly know everyone else). This lesson of adaptation is implicit in the structure and is not the actual focus of instruction. This latter, as with the rest of the exercises, is the subject of the teacher's presentations.

As presented, this activity is not based on course-specific material.

## Organization

Each person will be responsible for presenting an assigned chapter to a group. The chapter, dates, and groups are listed below.

Each presentation will consist of teaching, homework, and an essay. The teaching assignment is an entire chapter and will take place for two days.

The homework will be a different research discussion question to be assigned to each student for each day by the presenter. (Both questions are to be assigned the day before the presentations; thus, 8-10 questions will be assigned, depending on group size.) These questions will require reading and thinking about specific parts of the chapter and are meant to provoke analysis, opinion, controversy, or extension of ideas. Each student will then be prepared and required to speak 2-3 minutes on his or her research the next day. The presenter will fit these into the presentation as he or she sees fit.

On the third day each presenter will give an essay question on which the group will write for the entire period. This question must integrate the key concepts and main ideas of the chapter. It should be worded so that it asks for information that was presented in the presentation (including students' minipresentations) and also requires that the student take that information and speculate beyond the boundaries of the chapter.

The presenter and students will be graded on several scales simultaneously (described later).

To prevent the possibility of group stagnation and to allow meeting new people continually, the group membership will change after each presentation (after every three days).

A number of class periods will be devoted to preparation.

Each group will have a group leader.

## Grades

Grades will be given by the group teachers, the students, the class teacher, and the group leaders. The group teacher will grade and comment on the essay (fifty points) and grade each 2-3-minute minispeech (ten points each day). Students will grade and evaluate the presenter (100 points for the entire presentation). The class teacher will grade the student-teachers' presentations (100 points). The group leaders will give a participation grade for each student, not including the mini-speech (five points each day).

All grade sheets, except those for the essays, will be passed in to the class teacher after each student-teacher's round (i.e., every three days). The essay sheets are required three days after the essay.

The evaluation sheets provided with the exercise are designed as a gentle prodding toward evaluative thinking. The criteria for evaluation are listed in order to direct the students' minds into evaluative thinking. The numbered scale asks for a quantitative judgment for each criterion, and the comments section asks that this judgment be backed up with a rationale for the score. The combination of these aspects ensures that enough thought will be given to the evaluation that the students will indeed practice the skill while simultaneously helping improve the skills of others.

## Assignments

The student-teacher's assignment is to: (1) present the entire chapter, (2) assign (the day before presentation) the questions for both days (to be prepared before the presentation), (3) prepare an essay question before giving the presentation so that he or she can teach toward it, (4) grade student mini-speeches, and (5) grade essays and comment.

The students' assignment is to: (1) read (browse or skim) the chapter being presented, (2) prepare a 2-3-minute answer to the homework question each day, (3) write an essay on the third day of the chapter presentation, and (4) grade and evaluate the student-teacher.

The group leaders' assignment is to: (1) give participation grades for each student each day and (2) provide direction and motivation and keep up group morale, if necessary.

Presentation Chapters and Dates

| Assigned group member number | Chapter | Topic | Dates |
|---|---|---|---|
| 1 | 6 | socialization | 18, 19, 20 |
| 2 | 14 | family | 21, 22, Apr. 1 |
| 3 | 15 | education | 2, 3, 4 |
| 4 | 16 | religion | 5, 8, 9 |
| 5 | 17 | politics | 10, 11, 12 |
| 6 | 18 | work | 15, 16, 17 |

# Group Membership and Rotation

The following list is for group configuration for the first day only.

According to the sequence for rotation (shown after the list) for each student's group number (next to each student's name), students are to calculate the letter of their group for five repetitions of the indicated rotation. They will put these five letters next to their name. These are their groups for the next five presentations. For the first presentation, students are in the group in which their name is listed below.

*Group Membership*

A
1. Andreas
2. Astrid
3. Jenny F.
4. Shawn
5. Andy
6. Brian

B
1. Mary G.
2. Mary Beth
3. Nicole
4. Nancy
5. John P.
6. Margaret

C
1. Elaina
2. Laurie
3. Dana G.
4. Peggy
5. Jennifer P.
6. Denise

D
1. Karen
2. Sheri
3. Dana H.
4. Lisa L.
5. Kim
6. Kristin

E
1. John S.
2. Jenny E.
3. Jeff
4. Jody
5. Sheryl
6. Lisa Li.

*Sequence for Rotation*

| Group Member Number | Rotation |
|---|---|
| 1 | Stay (group leader) |
| 2 | 1 clockwise |
| 3 | 1 counterclockwise |
| 4 | 2 clockwise |
| 5 | 2 counterclockwise |
| 6 | 1 clockwise, 2 clockwise, 1 counterclockwise, 3 counterclockwise, 1 counterclockwise |

For example, if a student is number 2 and he or she is in group B on the list, his or her groups will be C, D, E, A, and B respectively. If a student is number 6 in this same group, his or her successive groups will be C, E, D, A, E.

The rotation serves many purposes. First, it prevents cliques from forming within groups. Second, it introduces everyone to everyone else. Third, it adds variety, excitement, and an element of the unknown to every day; no group gets too set into a routine and a pecking order. Fourth, it exposes everyone to all ability levels and gives everyone someone else with whom to identify. In this same vein, it helps everyone feel that they are not so very different from everyone else and that they are all in this together. Fifth, it makes grading democratic and prevents students from being victimized by one or two others.

Last, it fosters experimentation. It is difficult, for example, for a shy person to break out of his or her shell in a group that has already labeled him or her as shy. After a few presentations, however, this person might feel like trying to contribute more and will be able to do so without being embarrassed in attempting to escape from the confines of his or her label in front of the labelers. Fear of failure in front of those who have judged you is a powerful, inertia-laden emotion. On the other hand, experimentation in front of those the shy person does not know and who do not expect anything yet risks little, for he or she can always fall back into the "I knew I couldn't do it" posture.

Of course, some people react in just the opposite manner—they do not break out of their shells until they know people well, trust them, and like them. For these people, the stationary group activities are more apt to be successful, assuming that there is a good chemistry in that group.

**Figure 10.1.** *Teacher Evaluation*

|  | First day | Second day | Total |
|---|---|---|---|
| 1. Covered all the material in chapter<br>Comment: | 1 2 3 4 5 | 1 2 3 4 5 | _____ |
| 2. Filled the entire day's time period<br>(subtract 3 points for every 5 minutes<br>short)<br>Comment: | 1 2 3 4 5 | 1 2 3 4 5 | _____ |
| 3. Spoke from outline using own words<br>(not a written speech or from a<br>book)<br>Comment: | 1 2 3 4 5 | 1 2 3 4 5 | _____ |
| 4. Offered examples of concepts<br>Comment: | 1 2 3 4 5 | 1 2 3 4 5 | _____ |
| 5. Showed logical organization<br>with good use of time and materials<br>Comment: | 1 2 3 4 5 | 1 2 3 4 5 | _____ |
| 6. Included all members with research<br>questions and integrated those<br>minipresentations into the<br>overall presentation | 1 2 3 4 5 | 1 2 3 4 5 | _____ |
| 7. Offered analysis, opinion, and<br>different viewpoints to the<br>information given in the book<br>Comment: | 1 2 3 4 5 | 1 2 3 4 5 | _____ |
| 8. Explained each concept in<br>addition to simply telling you<br>what it is<br>Comment: | 1 2 3 4 5 | 1 2 3 4 5 | _____ |

9. Summarized, reworded, and
   elaborated on important concepts        1 2 3 4 5  1 2 3 4 5 _____
   Comment:

**Figure 10.2.** *Evaluations for Group Members*

This sheet is to be attached to each person's essay and turned in to the class teacher no later than three days after the essay is written.

Teacher _____
Student _____

Grading for minipresentations

|  | Day 1 | Day 2 | Total |
|---|---|---|---|
| 1. Did the group members research the homework assignment well? | 1 2 3 4 | 1 2 3 4 | _____ |
| 2. Did they spend 2-3 minutes on the presentation? | 1 2 3 4 | 1 2 3 4 | _____ |
| 3. Did they speak in their own words instead of reading from the book? | 1 2 3 4 | 1 2 3 4 | _____ |
| Total | _____ | _____ | |

Grading for Esays
1. Each presenter must read, grade, and comment (where appropriate) on the essays of all group members These grade sheet will be attached to the essay and handed in to the class teacher.
2. You have three days after the essay is written to hand them in.
3. The class teacher will enter the grades and hand back to all students.

Criteria:
1. Did the group members answer
   what the question asked?        1 2 3 4 5 6 7 8 9 10 _____
   Comment:

2. Did they use adequate information
   from your presentation in their
   argument?                                1 2 3 4 5 6 7 8 9 10 _____
   Comment:
3. Did they support their arguments
   or statements with facts, examples,
   and justifications, or did they simply make statements without
   proof?                                   1 2 3 4 5 6 7 8 9 10 _____
   Comment:
4. Did their analysis probe beneath
   the surface and simple common
   sense to interesting, unique,
   or profound observations?                1 2 3 4 5 6 7 8 9 10 _____
   Comment:
5. Was the argument well organized
   and logical?                             1 2 3 4 5 6 7 8 9 10 _____
   Comment:

**Figure 10.8.** *Participation Grades for Group Members*

This grade is given by the group leader each day to each person.
It does not include the minispeeches.

Criteria:
 1. The participation grade is based on the number and quality of
    questions and contributions regarding subject matter or proce-
    dure.
 2. The grade must be scaled to the amount of participation per-
    mitted or required by the student-teacher.

Teacher _____

| Names | Day 1 | Day 2 | Total |
|---|---|---|---|
| 1. | 1 2 3 4 5 | 1 2 3 4 5 | _____ |
| 2. | 1 2 3 4 5 | 1 2 3 4 5 | _____ |
| 3. | 1 2 3 4 5 | 1 2 3 4 5 | _____ |
| 4. | 1 2 3 4 5 | 1 2 3 4 5 | _____ |
| 5. | 1 2 3 4 5 | 1 2 3 4 5 | _____ |
| 6. | 1 2 3 4 5 | 1 2 3 4 5 | _____ |

# 11

## Toward Multidimensional Teaching and Learning

So often we teachers lack an overall multidimensional lesson plan. A meaningful plan goes so much deeper than the facts that should be learned and the order of their presentation. All levels of human development must be planned into the lessons, not just some surface-level indicator of what we hope is going on behind the scenes.

The ideas presented here can be put to this purpose in many different ways and be used to develop a program of teaching students to teach themselves. The exercises presented here can be improved, expanded, and added to; they are simply first steps to a new beginning.

The multidimensional nature of this teaching approach will add fresh insights into behavior, learning, and teaching. It will give a new direction, integration, and scope to all teaching, as well as introduce a substructural glue that will hold everything together in a focused, consistent and reinforcing pattern.

Some levels at which multidimensional planning aims are not as predictable and measurable as others. The outcomes may evolve slowly and be a surprise to everyone. This unpredictability should not deter us, and we must take aim, plan, organize, and teach to every level. One level without the others is not enough on which to build a whole person.

The amount of learning that can be accomplished with activities such as these is enormous. The only limits are the teacher's creativity and ability to orchestrate all that is going on, but these, too, will grow. This role is different from those teachers are used to—instead of being on center stage, we are backstage, but we are doing the directing. As much or more planning will be necessary, but it is of a much different nature. Instead of preparing a lecture about facts that we already know, we are constantly creating, looking for new relationships, seeking new ways to organize, and integrating numerous pieces into a coherent whole. This act of creating adds excitement, variety, and a feeling of empowerment and self-expression to our job—the same sensations that we are trying to stimulate in students.

As students' skills develop, so must our lessons and the structure of the activities. The abilities that lie fallow now are soon to be developed, and we and the class will be propelled onto a whole new level of classroom possibility. We have to evolve also. We have to become aware of new levels of thinking, new directions, new possibilities, and new kinds of thought—all uncharted territory for the classroom.

This book presents a method of reorienting our perspective on the true meaning of teaching and learning and how they are accomplished. Many solutions to our education problems, some of which go as far as totally revamping or dismantling our present school system, have been proposed in the past. For now, however, we must accept that the school system is with us for a while but that within this system changes can be made and with almost no upheaval in the present administration and structure. Simply with a change in perspective and teaching techniques within the classroom, giant strides forward can be made in altering the learning environment and the results. We can accomplish our ultimate educational objective of making a major contribution to the development of fully actualized individuals instead of perpetuating the myth that that is what we presently do with our current techniques. These, when examined appear instead to be anathema to those very goals. This book is one first step toward eliminating that incongruity.

371.102
L752

LINCOLN CHRISTIAN COLLEGE AND SEMINARY 80202